The
EVERYTHIN
Guide to Raising Adolescent Boys

Dear Reader,

I love being the mother of boys! From day one, my sons have been so different from my daughters. Raising them has been a very welcome challenge. When they were younger, the differences were all about trucks, mud pies, and energy levels. Today the differences are a bit harder to detect, but still so very important. The privacy issues, the school issues—there are days it can seem like an endless challenge. But at the end of the day, their love is so wonderful.

I admit to worrying about so many of the pitfalls that face today's youth. There are all the normal things we thought we'd be worried about as parents, like drugs, alcohol, and sex. But for parents nowadays, it also seems that we need to have an advanced degree in technology to monitor our children's schoolwork and social lives, and a degree in psychology to help figure out half of what our sons are saying. I have learned to believe that navigating through the tumult is half the fun of raising boys. They always keep you guessing.

As your son grows, I wish you the sense of peace and enjoyment that can come from being the parent of a son. Remember that you are his first and most impressive teacher.

Robin Elise Weiss

The EVERYTHING® Series

These handy, accessible books give you all you need to tackle a difficult project, gain a new hobby, or even brush up on something you learned back in school but have since forgotten. You can read cover to cover or just pick out information from the four useful boxes.

Ⓔ Alerts: Urgent warnings

Ⓔ Essentials: Quick handy tips

Ⓔ Facts: Important snippets of information

Ⓔ Questions: Answers to common questions

When you're done reading, you can finally say you know EVERYTHING®!

DIRECTOR OF INNOVATION Paula Munier

EDITORIAL DIRECTOR Laura M. Daly

EXECUTIVE EDITOR, SERIES BOOKS Brielle K. Matson

ASSOCIATE COPY CHIEF Sheila Zwiebel

ACQUISITIONS EDITOR Kerry Smith

ASSOCIATE DEVELOPMENT EDITOR Elizabeth Kassab

PRODUCTION EDITOR Casey Ebert

Visit the entire Everything® series at *www.everything.com*

THE
EVERYTHING®
GUIDE TO
RAISING
ADOLESCENT
BOYS

WITHDRAWN

Reassuring advice to help you and
your son navigate these turbulent years

Robin Elise Weiss, LCCE
with Mary E. Muscari, Ph.D., R.N.

Aadamsmedia
avon, massachusetts

*To Benjamin and Isaac, who have taught me everything
I needed know about being the mother of a boy.*

• • •

An Everything® Series Book.
Everything® and everything.com® are registered
trademarks of F+W Publications, Inc.

Published by Adams Media, an F+W Publications Company
57 Littlefield Street, Avon, MA 02322 U.S.A.
www.adamsmedia.com

ISBN 10: 1-59869-461-8
ISBN 13: 978-1-59869-461-1

Printed in the United States of America.

J I H G F E D C B A

Library of Congress Cataloging-in-Publication Data
is available from the publisher.

*This book is available at quantity discounts for bulk purchases.
For information, please call 1-800-289-0963.*

Acknowledgments

Writing this book was a lot of fun and truly helped me explore my parenting at its most intimate level. There were many people who helped keep me sane, knowledgeable, inspired, and on task: Mari Yesowitch Hopkins, Pat Predmore, Teri Shilling, Denise Witmer, Heather Levinson, and Mary Jo Podgursky. I also need to thank Barbara Doyen, Kerry Smith, and Dr. Mary Muscari for their technical assistance as I wrote this book. My husband provided me with a bird's-eye view of being a boy. I think he enjoyed reliving his youth and having an excuse to tell me about all the wild things he did as a teen for the sake of research. And a very special thanks to my son Benjamin for being my personal assistant while I wrote—your assistance was invaluable.

Contents

Introduction

Boys are different from girls. While this is not a surprise, it is not simply a matter of body parts; it encompasses the mind, emotions, and other aspects of a person. Adolescent boys in particular present unique challenges to their parents. To be the most effective parent, you will need to know different mechanisms for raising your son.

Parenting your son is one of the most challenging and rewarding jobs you will ever have. It means you will spend countless nights up with him or wondering about him—even after infancy. Picking up this book, maybe you thought about the relationship you hope for with your son. Being an effective parent is about learning and growing along with your son.

Your son has a lot to do in the years between his thirteenth and eighteenth birthdays. He has to learn to be with a crowd and yet still be an individual. He has to get ready to be on his own and grasp the responsibilities of budgeting, earning, and dealing with money. He has to shop for food, do his laundry, and clean up his own messes.

The Everything® Guide to Raising Adolescent Boys will help you in your quest to ensure that you are on top of all the things you need to know about raising a strong, confident son. You will learn how to talk to your son about difficult topics like sex and drug abuse. You will find the answers to your pressing questions on how to prevent your son from being violent or becoming a victim of violence. You will see how your son will differ from a daughter and figure out how to decide what is normal and what is not normal so that you might seek the appropriate help for him.

By being a more effective parent, you can help your son be a self-assured, valuable member of society while still maintaining his individuality. You will be able to lessen the number of arguments you have with your son and learn to deal with potential negativity and bad attitudes in the most effective manner.

Learning to deal with all the details of being a boy will give you the insight to help your son make decisions that will help him be an upstanding citizen and member of your family. You can work with your son to show him how to grow and mature to be the man you hope him to be.

Because of your involved parenting style, your son will learn to look forward to the future and find a path that is the most appropriate for him. You will find ways to ensure that you have a long and healthy relationship with your son far into the future. The parenting that you do for your son today will be the parenting that takes him through the hardest parts of his life and will help him become a more effective parent to his own children.

Chapter 1

Definition of
Adolescent Boys

Snakes and snails and puppy-dog tails notwithstanding, teenage boys are an enigma. One minute they are fun and friendly, the next minute they are incredibly moody and sullen. Your son will go from being a boy to a man in just a short span of years—emotionally and physically. You are your son's greatest asset during this time.

Being a Boy

Boys are not a one size fits all. You can't simply parent every single boy in the same manner. You have to remember that your son is an individual.

The All-American Boy

From the moment someone said, "It's a boy!" you've probably had an inkling of what that meant. Your dream son had good grades, a nice after-school job, and a sweet girlfriend. He did everything he was told and never talked back, though his room was a bit messy. Wake up call! Umpteen years later, that boy doesn't exist, except in the imaginations of his parents.

Your Son, the Individual

Your adolescent son is special—at least he thinks so. Every action he takes may be new to him, but that doesn't mean they haven't been done before. This can be a huge shock. His individuality can help or hinder his growth. You need to see him as an individual. Give him space to be himself.

The Difference a Year Makes

As soon as your son entered middle school, you probably started to notice dramatic changes. Each year from here on out creates even more drastic changes.

Physical Growth

Your thirteen-year-old son may look tiny to you, nowhere near what you'd expect a man to look like. Give him five years, and he will be very manlike.

 Fact

A study by the Virginia Tech Cooperative Extension showed teen boys can gain an average of 4.1 inches in height from a one-year growth spurt. That's a lot of new pants! Girls hit this growth spurt about two years before boys, so if your son is shorter than his current love interest, tell him not to panic.

Watching your son change literally overnight can send parents into a tizzy. Try to remember your son is looking to you for comfort, strength, and knowledge.

Emotional Growth

You may not expect the mental and emotional changes that come with adolescence. Mood swings occur in boys during puberty. This too shall pass, but hang on for a wild ride.

Ⓔ *Essential*

Teen Growth (*www.teengrowth.com*) is a site that offers some great articles for boys and their parents. The topics are mostly health-based, but it also offers some fun things like a growth calculator to help you predict your son's adult height.

You may not know whether you'll be met with a snarling teenager or a mild-mannered boy when you try to speak to your son. No matter how your son responds to you, it is important to keep the lines of communication open. Be sure to find the pattern that helps you talk to him best. Remember that growing up is hard for him as well. Try to sit him down to explain what's going on; this may help you both prevent that overwhelming feeling and it makes for a nice reality check.

The Eating and Sleeping Machine

During adolescence, your son is likely to grow four to twelve inches and gain between fifteen and sixty-five pounds. As your son grows, his needs change. Your son will exhibit dramatic changes in the way he approaches eating and sleeping; they may seem to dominate his life, and you may feel they are all he does day in and day out. Never fear—it's normal.

How Can You Feed This Boy?

Growing boys simply require a lot of fuel to keep them going. Think of everything going on in his body—the muscle expansion, the gain in height, and the internal changes.

 Fact

As a parent, you might cringe to think of the amount of calories your son consumes on a daily basis. For most boys, the body will burn all of the calories in the course of playing, exercising, and growing. A noticeable weight gain means you need to evaluate your son's lifestyle and food choices.

In addition to keeping the house well stocked with food, adolescence is a time of great learning potential. Your son can learn to help cook for himself. You can foster his good eating choices by ensuring that there are always health alternatives in the house. It's a good idea to stock up on quick food items, like fresh fruits and vegetables that your son can easily grab to snack on.

Sleep

Between nine and ten hours of sleep is a nice average for an adolescent boy, though this can be a battle. Your son will often resist both going to bed and waking up. As adults, parents see the whole cycle, but your son only understands the instant benefit of his desire—either staying awake or staying asleep. While you can try to remind him that getting up will be much easier if he goes to bed now, it may not sink in. This is definitely one area where rules and consequences are best applied.

Ⓔ *Essential*

Try to find a schedule that works well for your son. Experiment with different bedtimes and wake times. Your son can tell you how he's feeling as he tries the different routines. You should also consider a bedtime routine.

A study in *Child Development* showed that adolescent boys who don't get enough sleep are more likely to have bad grades, be depressed, or have other negative effects from sleep deprivation. The irony is that your son's increased need for sleep corresponds with an increased need for him to be awake more in order to fully participate in his activities.

Physical Changes

To say that puberty is a time of physical change is like saying that the ocean has some water in it. While you can't predict exactly when puberty will occur or exactly how it will affect your son, having lots of information on puberty can help soften the blow for both you and your son.

Welcome to Your New Body

Puberty starts differently for different boys. Some boys seem to hit puberty a bit earlier than others, but in general, it starts between the ages of ten and sixteen. The first thing that most parents and boys notice may be body growth, specifically in the extremities. Your son's arms, legs, hands, and feet may seem suddenly enormous compared to the rest of his body.

 Fact

Your son should know not only about male puberty, but also about what females go through. The American Academy of Pediatrics has an informational Web site with information for boys and girls at *www.aap.org/family/puberty.htm*.

When you notice other physical changes, you may also notice an increase in muscles or muscle definition. You will notice an increase in your son's appetite. Once he has started to develop muscle, he may be interested in lifting weights. Clear it with your child's health care practitioner. This can help prevent damage to newly developed muscles.

Surface Changes

Acne. It's a huge way that the skin changes in puberty and the teenage years. Acne is caused by changes in the production of oil on the skin, usually around the face and neck area.

ⓔ *Essential*

Many young men experience soreness or swelling near their nipples. Assure your son that this does not mean he is growing breasts. Sometimes small circular band-aids, worn over the nipples, help with shirts that irritate the skin.

Your son's body will also develop hair. He will find that he has hair under his arms, his face, his legs, his groin, and his chest. Some boys find it uncomfortable and itchy. You may notice your son sweats more and that he smells as well. This is a good time to introduce deodorant.

During puberty, your son's voice will change. It will crack as your son's voice shifts from a higher register to a lower one. Eventually the cracking will stop, and your son's voice will be permanently lower. He may be embarrassed at first, as he has no control over this change.

Emotional Changes

As with the growth your son's body undergoes, his emotions also change. This may mean mood swings as he adjusts to his hormones. It is also important to note how your son's experiences and relationships with others will change.

Relationships

As your son grows emotionally, his relationships will change to reflect that. In some cases, old friendships may die out. This is a natural process, whether it happens through a large fight or gradual, mutual neglect that leads to both parties finding other friends.

 Fact

Egocentric thinking starts in infancy. While it does go away eventually, growing out of it is a learning process. This change starts to happen for most boys in early adolescence. It can have a drastic effect on your son's relationships.

You may find that your son wants to be with adults more frequently. This may fulfill his desire to be older and show off his newfound maturity. It can be helpful if he finds a mentor, but it can also be a negative thing. You need to monitor any relationships your son has with other adults to make sure there are no inappropriate interactions.

Romantic Relations

It was once thought that young men weren't romantically inclined. Sure, they dated, but it was the girls that had all the feelings. Boys could simply date around and it wouldn't matter with whom they spent time or what happened when it was over because they approached relationships as emotionless hormone-crazed beings. A 2006 study published in *American Sociological Review* turns this theory on its head.

This study showed that boys are just as emotionally invested as girls in their early romantic relationships. It demonstrated that young men do have their hearts in their relationships and don't date simply to meet their physical needs. In fact, it showed that adolescent girls tend to wield more power than their boyfriends in making decisions in relationships, including decisions about sex. Regardless of gender, the study reported that puppy love isn't as insignificant as it is often portrayed. Early relationships are valuable experiences that teach boys how to conduct themselves and help shape future relationships. This study also documented how awkward it is for young men to talk about their relationships. It may be doubly hard for you to get your son to open up; he may not feel it's any of your business, and he's uncomfortable talking about it anyway.

Thinking Changes

In his adolescent years, your son's way of thinking will change. He will learn to think in the abstract. He will form his own ideas, and he will explore complex thinking.

Complex Ways to Think

One of the biggest changes to your son's thinking is the ability to consider multiple factors when making a decision. He will be able to consider your thoughts, the perceived ramifications at school or home, and his own opinions and desires, all in one complex process.

As your son begins to grasp more complex thinking, he will also start to look to the future and how his current decisions may affect his future goals. In addition to thinking of his future, he will also learn to consider the welfare of other people, including thinking on a national or international level, something a new teen can't typically begin to do.

Fact

Parents often find themselves frustrated when their sons simply can't seem to manage to do more than one thing at a time. Recent imaging data shows us that the portion of the brain that handles multitasking doesn't fully develop until after puberty.

Encouraging Cognitive Growth

You are a big influence on your son's thinking and cognitive development. Your goal is to help him learn these thought processes as he develops. Include your son in adult conversations. Discuss local politics, talk about current events, find something that is important to him, and encourage him to express his opinion verbally in front of the family.

Goal setting is another way to incorporate future thinking. Have your son talk about his future goals. Encourage him to write these down and address the steps that need to be met in order for those goals to happen. This will give him a sense of ownership over his thoughts and decisions.

Chapter 2

Parenting Boys

Unfortunately, your son did not come with an instruction manual. Never fear! Raising a boy is not as difficult as it can seem. The key is putting forth a good effort as a parent and learning as you go. Parenting is the perfect on-the-job training, and it need not be defined by stress and conflict.

How Boys Are Different

From the moment he was born, society began to exert pressure on your son to fit a certain model of masculinity. While boys do have certain innate abilities and desires, this does not mean you have no influence as a parent. In fact, your job is to act as a buffer for your son.

Being Masculine

You see them on television and driving down the street: signs that show your son how he is supposed to act to be a man. These commercials, movies, books, and magazine ads are just one part of the problem. Society also plays a big role in enforcing these stereotypes such as: Boys roughhouse, and your son should play with trucks, not dolls.

Emotional and physical growth paints only a small portion of the overall picture of the innate differences between boys and girls. While it is not imperative that you understand and list every difference, the point is that the differences are there. As a parent, you must learn to determine how these differences matter to your child. Your son will spend the rest of his life doing the same thing without even knowing it.

 Fact

The *Journal of Individual Differences* studied how boys and girls coped. Girls scored higher in seeking social support, while boys scored higher in avoidance activities. Help your son learn about social support and the dangers of avoidance.

Cultural messages can be overwhelming. While it is important to help shield your son from them in some respects, it is also important to acknowledge that these influences do matter and that they do have a point. But your son needs to learn how to incorporate his own identity with that identity from society. Allowing him the flexibility to be himself is what adolescence is about. How he does this will be a personal journey that you can help guide, though not live, for your son.

Boys Need a Male Influence

Growing up as a boy is hard enough with two parents. If your son is growing up in a single-parent home, for whatever reason, this journey will be more difficult. If this home doesn't have a male in it, your son's growth will be more difficult. Boys need a male mentor.

This male can be your son's biological father, but he doesn't have to be. There are other places to try to help your son find masculine role models. This might be a program that offers older male mentors to young boys, though these programs are often full and have wait lists. You might also have another male relative who can help you by spending time with your son.

Single Children

The stereotypical attitude of an only child is not a pretty one. You often hear words like snotty, spoiled, and bratty bandied about to describe only children. The good news is that research says that these descriptions are, for the most part, myths.

Only children scored similarly to firstborn children in research on the differences between the two groups. Only children scored well in social skills as well as in achievement scores, breaking old myths about only childhood being a disease.

This is not to say that only children have it easy. There is more that you need to focus on as a parent of any only child. Your son may have the benefits of the attention of both parents, but you need to make sure you allow your son to experience life. One problem with only children tends to be that the parents can be over-involved. This means their son is not allowed to "fight" for himself.

Peer interactions and friends are important to the only child. This is where he will learn to play nicely with others and to behave in a group. When you as a parent step in to help your son play, he misses an opportunity to learn to deal with others. By the time your son is a teen, this can mean your son is closer to the stereotypes of only children than he should be.

 Fact

Your son may ask why he is an only child. How you answer will be based on his age and why he is asking. At age thirteen, he may not need to know the details of your finances or your reproductive health, but when he's older it may be something you feel more like sharing.

Having Siblings

Siblings form a special bond. Hopefully, that bond winds up being one of friendship and family ties, but don't panic if peace and harmony don't reign over your children's lives in the teen years. This is normal and should pass.

They Are All Special

Each of your children is special. Each has his or her own talents, abilities, and personality. This is what you need to focus on as a parent.

By focusing on these differences, you can help each of your children grow to his strengths. This doesn't mean your son won't ever accuse you of treating his siblings better. That's a part of life, and it's easy for a teen to try to manipulate his parents through guilt. Each child will have times when he needs more of your time and attention. This is normal.

When your children fight, talk to your son about what it will be like when he grows up. Explain to him how siblings, while annoying now, are potentially the most wonderful family he will have when he is grown. They share the common bond of the same family story as well as similar values. This is a built-in community, no matter how far apart they are from one another. The fights today are the friendships tomorrow.

E *Alert*

If your son is very distant from his siblings in age, he may seem more like an only child. Take the initiative to keep him connected to his siblings: have an older son read to younger siblings or have him attend events for younger siblings.

Sibling Rivalry

Siblings offer a great opportunity to learn about emotions—positive and negative. Fighting is part of the territory. You need to decide how to handle it and stick to your guns.

Will you allow them to fight? You may not have much of a choice. Do you really want to be judge and jury? Probably not. The important thing is to make it clear that you refuse to take part in their fights. Fights for attention should stop pretty soon. Fights sometimes do become physical. If they become violent and include items like knives, it is important to get counseling for your children and family to help resolve what is not normal sibling rivalry.

ⒺＥssential

One study in *Child Development* showed that the key to preventing sibling conflict and rivalry may be treating each child differently. This means that you should spend time doing something special with each of your children alone.

Birth Order

Birth order is a way to help categorize your son's behavior and attitude based on where he was born in the family. Sex, age, and child spacing can influence birth-order effects. This can be very helpful to some parents and not so helpful to others.

What Is Birth Order?

Birth order defines one's personality and psychological relationships based on the rank and order of one's birth compared to one's siblings. This is to say that a firstborn child will be different from a second-born, purely because he is the firstborn. This has become a very popular theory in psychology.

You may read issues related to birth order and feel like someone has been spying on your home. You or your child may fit perfectly into the described behaviors and attitudes of your birth order. Other parents may look at birth order and find that it doesn't really hold true for their family. Either way, the information on how to deal with different personalities can be helpful, even if they don't match the order of birth.

The Personalities

The firstborn child is said to be the leader of the family. Traits and attitudes assigned to the first-born include:

- Nervousness
- High achievement
- Aggressiveness
- Rule-orientation
- Detail-orientation

Parents supposedly worry more over a firstborn because of their status as new parents. They worry about everything and pressure their child to succeed.

Middle children are supposed to have more flexible personalities. They may be good communicators and negotiators because of their place between siblings. This gives them a unique perspective and a chance to mediate. A middle child may also learn to fight for the little person in life.

 Fact

It is important to remember that not every child fits nicely into the categories defined by any theory. In the end you really have to get to know your own children to determine if this information is helpful to you in parenting.

The youngest child is the baby of the family. The baby may turn out to be a good friend and a charmer—but on the flip side, he may also manipulate to get what he wants.

Twins also are affected by birth order, though according to Clifford Isaacson, the actual order of birth is not as much of a factor here. The twin with the dominant personality must work harder to dominate a twin of the same skill sets.

Remember that these are just the basics. Birth order may not affect your children as much as others. Your children are individuals and should be treated as such.

E Fact

Other adults in your son's life will also be role models for him. It is important to screen these people as much as possible. Try to enroll him in programs that have positive male role models.

Parent as Role Model

Probably not a day goes by that you don't question whether you are meeting your goals. When you are talking about a teen boy, it is even more difficult to feel like you are hitting that good-parent mark. The truth is that being a good parent involves many different paths and ideas, and choosing which path is the hard part, particularly when you have to deal with the input of your teen. The easiest way to reach your teen is to be a good role model.

Being a Role Model

The stress of trying to be a role model weighs heavily on some people. This may make you feel like you simply can't be yourself around your child. Nothing could be further from the truth. Your child will love you no matter what you do, just as you will always love him.

If you want your son to grow up with the values and belief systems you possess, the easiest way to teach him those values is to show him what they look like in action. Show him you are a good friend by treating your own friends well. Show him you believe in your country by showing him how you participate in voting and political endeavors. Provide him with instructional mini-lessons in being a good person.

E Essential

Learning the lingo your son uses online and in text messaging can help you be aware of what's going on and win you bonus points for being clued in. There are many sites available to help you figure out what's going on.

If you find that your son has different opinions, embrace them. Doing so can spark a healthy discussion, which may help both of you grow in your convictions, even if you do not share them. Change is not always fun, but it is necessary.

Don't Panic

Mistakes happen. This is true for adults as well as kids. Simply because you are a parent doesn't mean you are immune from making mistakes. In fact, you might make more. The difference is how you handle them.

By acknowledging your mistakes and dealing with the consequences, you teach your son a very valuable lesson. He will see how a grownup responds to mistakes. He will see you took responsibility and tried to correct the problem. This is a very valuable lesson in the teen years, where the urge to cover up mistakes and ignore them is natural.

Chapter 3

Staying Connected with Your Son

The teen years are particularly hard when it comes to communicating with your son. Not only is he physically gone from your home more, but when he is home, he may be more inclined to chat with his friends online or on the phone than to speak to you. This means that establishing a foundation for good communication is essential.

Communication Skills for Parents of Teens

Communicating with a teen can be a problem for many parents. You might feel like you don't speak his language or that he doesn't understand you. There are ways to help fight this feeling and have adequate and even meaningful discussions.

How to Listen

It may surprise you to see that listening is listed first. But it is the most important skill you can possess when talking to your teenaged son, or anyone for that matter. Parents not listening is one of the biggest complaints made by teens when it comes to talking to their parents and other adults.

E Essential

Be mindful of your body language. If you assume a posture that says, "I'm not listening" or "I'm angry," your son will shut you out. Look at your son, tilting your head slightly. Nod at the appropriate points. Show him you are really listening.

There are a few simple tricks to learn about listening. The first is simply to give your child your full attention. This may mean stopping what you're doing to provide him that attention. You should also look at your son while he is speaking to you and when you are speaking to him. Eye contact is respectful and shows you are paying attention.

While he speaks, actually listen to what your son is saying. Many times parents have a problem because they either interrupt or plan what they will say next instead of truly listening. When your son is finished talking, pause to reflect on what he said. Then you should restate what he has said and ask if you understood. Allow your son to correct anything you misunderstood.

Listening is an active skill. You need to be there with your son, interpreting everything that goes into his conversation. Note how he sits, what his body language says, what words he chooses, and what tone he uses. Remember to refrain from judgment.

How to Send a Clear Message

Feeling misunderstood is a universal theme of being a teenager. The problem is that when you're the parent of a teen, you want him to hear and understand what you are saying.

 *Alert*

Most teens prefer to talk to their mothers about tough issues. Try to feel your son out to see which parent he is more responsive to, but remember to present a united front in terms of your message to him.

No matter what you're doing, make a list and check it twice to ensure you are giving your son the correct information and he understands it. Writing gives him a chance to slow down to read instructions and ask questions before starting. If he forgets a step, he has a backup plan in the written document.

To-do lists can make great contracts for dealing with some tougher issues. You might make a long-term agreement over grades. If he gets X grades for Y period of time, then you will reward him with Z. Be sure you both sign and date it.

Finding a Time and Place to Talk

One of the hardest things to do is to find just the right time and place to talk with your son. Don't assume you can have any conversation anywhere at any time. The right time and place can actually make or break your conversation.

Is There Ever a Good Time?

There are days when you may feel like you have not seen your son at all; indeed, you may not have. If you have busy or opposite schedules, it's entirely possible to go a day without seeing him even if you live in the same house. While this should be the exception to the rule, it does occasionally happen.

 **Essential**

Let your son know what you want to talk to him about. If you don't, you may make him worry needlessly until the appointed time. If you can't really say what it's about, be sure to let him know he is not in trouble.

Scheduling a good time to talk provides you both with ample time to have the conversation. Some conversations are five minutes long; others may last a lot longer. Keep this in mind when picking a time to talk.

You will need to look to your son for his best times to talk. Very few teenaged boys are morning people, so avoid times of day when he is not at his best. One or both of you may actually have to alter your schedule to make a discussion happen. If you wait for the exact perfect time to talk, you may never find it—a good alternative could be to orchestrate a situation that is as close to ideal as possible.

Where Not to Talk

While a good conversation can happen almost anywhere, there are a few places that are not conducive to meaningful talks. Avoid places where your son's friends will be around, unless they need to be a part of the conversation. School functions, sporting events, and other social venues are the wrong place to discuss anything of substance. You may also need to avoid having important discussions in earshot of some family members, particularly eavesdropping younger siblings.

Avoid places where your son may feel he doesn't have an equal footing. Sitting in the living room feels very different from sitting in your office with you behind your desk. The latter gives you the upper hand. Neutral places that often work well include the park, small cafés, the car, or other places where you are not near friends or family and yet your son will not feel you are trying to dominate or intimidate him.

What Not to Do

When talking to your teen, there are a list of taboos that you will need to keep in mind. Most of them are common sense, and you follow them in your daily conversations with others, so they should not be too difficult to apply in conversations with your son.

Don't Say That!

One of the hardest parts of parenthood is putting your foot in your mouth. Sometimes you do this unknowingly, and other times you see it coming. Knowing what not to say to your son is just as important as knowing what to say and how to say it.

 **Alert**

Sarcasm, as easy as it can be for some parents to use, is not an appropriate tool for dealing with your teen son. Statements can too easily be misunderstood, and you may inadvertently hurt your son's feelings or alienate him.

It is important to not make empty threats to your son. Don't tell him you'll take away his driving privileges for a month if you know perfectly well you will be unable to drive him to all of his activities. Mean exactly what you say; this is a part of consistent parenting.

Do not lie to your son. If you promise something, you had better be sure you can fulfill that promise. If you are unsure of something, be honest and say that to your son.

Don't overstate matters. If you give your son a compliment, be sure it is real. Only when you state the facts without embellishment will your son be able to believe you.

Your son may be sensitive to other subjects or conversational quirks. By listening to your son, you will be able to figure these things out. Noticing his comfort level and taking it into account are part of good parenting.

Don't Miss Opportunities to Talk

It isn't uncommon for parents to feel like they've expended a great deal of effort to get a short conversation out of their son. The problem is that parents frequently miss those golden opportunities to talk to their son.

These conversations are usually at inconvenient times. It might be late at night when you're tired or just as you're about to head out the door for an important meeting, but usually it's a case of bad timing that causes parents to overlook these great opportunities. If you recognize it is time for a talk and you have other responsibilities, see if you can delay your other responsibility. Simply say to your son, "I care and want to talk now, let me call in to let them know I'm running late." This shows your son that you respect him and will take the time out but that you are also holding up your responsibilities.

 Fact

Sometimes talking while on a walk or in a car is a perfect opportunity. You're physically present but not face to face, which can be intimidating to teens. This is a great way to get your son to open up with minimal effort.

Another reason parents miss great opportunities to talk is because they don't recognize them. Your son might say something that is, in a very small way, an invitation to talk. It may seem very innocent, like "How was your day?" It might be an action, such as if he's hanging around the kitchen while you're cooking, or sitting in the room with you while you're watching television.

Finding these small times can open up some of the best opportunities for you to talk to your son. The more you're aware of what they look like, the more likely you are to find them. Keeping the lines of communication open is key to your relationship with your son.

Talking to Your Son

It may seem like he is talking to you less and less. Even if the quantity has changed, the quality is the most important aspect of talking to your son. You need to overcome your fears of tough topics in order to have the relationship and conversations he needs in order to grow into manhood.

Important Conversations

One of the things most parents do not realize is that every interaction with their son is important. He may end up remembering a conversation that you thought was completely inconsequential.

 *Essential*

It can be difficult for parents to talk with one voice, yet this is the very foundation of your parenting philosophy. To do this, you have to be sure you communicate well with your partner in parenting.

There are certain conversations you have to have with your son. Some of them are about how to live a good life. Other conversations will save him time and money. There are also conversations that may save his life.

Use Role-Play

Role-playing can help your teen see how different scenarios will play out in real life. This tool is probably one of the most underused parenting tools, yet it is wildly effective.

E Alert

Once he's in his mid-teens, talk to your son about his future. Ask him about his ideal career and what he needs to do to accomplish that goal. The Occupational Outlook Handbook at *www.bls.gov/oco/* can be of assistance.

You do not need to be a world famous actor to role-play effectively as a parent. You need to have at least a reasonable idea of what you're talking about and a willingness to listen and learn from your son.

You can be your son explaining a situation and let him play the teacher. This allows him to see the situation from his teacher's standpoint. He may choose to answer the situation with an appropriate answer, but if he doesn't, use the opportunity to step in and ask questions.

This technique is very handy when it comes to dealing with situations where your son needs to think. Role-playing peer relationships works very nicely. He may not realize how hard it can be when his friends say things he does not expect from them. Perhaps he can't imagine his friends ever smoking, and role-playing will help him conceptualize a situation and how to formulate an answer when you ask him what he will say if he is offered a cigarette.

Role-playing can be as serious or as silly as is appropriate for you and your son. Part of how silly it gets depends on the situation you are discussing, though it is important to realize that your son may act a bit silly as a coping mechanism.

 *Question*

Should I use text messages to talk with my son?
Text messaging can be a handy communication tool. It may be a nice way to have a conversation with your son because it takes away the potentially intimidating quality of a face-to-face conversation. However, it can become a problem if you begin to rely on it as a primary means of communication.

The Family Meal

Between after-school activities, late work days, and fast food, who has the time or inclination to make steak au poivre with a garden salad on a regular basis? That's the wrong question. You should ask yourself who needs the family meal. The answer, of course, is everyone.

A Great Ritual

The family meal provides an invaluable opportunity to gather at the end of a long day of study and work to eat and socialize with each other.

By getting together every day or most days of the week, you can actually find out a lot of information about how your son's life is going. It is a time to eat, yes, but it is also a time for your family members to talk about life. Some days the conversations may be lighthearted; other days they may be nonexistent, but stick with it.

 *Alert*

Taking the time to prepare and eat dinner with your family sends a message that you care. The time you take to reconnect shows your son, no matter how much he complains about it, that you care.

Think of the family meal as a time to take the emotional temperature of your family. Your son's moods and attitudes will tell you a lot about his day, even if he doesn't. Dinner gives you a chance to explore deeper, either during or after. It also gives him a chance to be with you in a safe environment. Dinner is a natural way to get the family together, a prescheduled, guaranteed time for everyone to meet. Eating together sends a message that you are spending time with your son because you want to.

Planning a Family Meal

Don't sweat having a family meal if you haven't done it in a while. All you do is pick a time, inform everyone of that time, and add food—instant family meal! Do not stress about what you're eating. It does not have to be a huge Thanksgiving-style dinner. It really is about the family.

E Essential

There are many products available to help your family have discussions at the table. Many are no larger than a deck of cards. Each card will contain a topic to start a discussion. Once you get the conversation going, it snowballs.

Expect that your family may buck at the idea of having to come to the table together if it is a new concept. Slowly integrating family night back into your lives naturally eases the transition.

Many families decide to make these nights sacred: to interfere with family dinner night is a huge deal. If something does come up, be flexible. Reschedule for a different night or evaluate whether the conflicting event can be postponed. Remember that your son may see things differently than you do, so this is one area to expect conflict.

Sitting around the table together may feel awkward at first. Start a conversation by asking what everyone did at school or work that day. If this elicits a bunch of "nothings," you may have to dig deeper. Some families play games while eating. One game, which works well for all ages, is to pick a letter and then go around the table and have everyone say a word that begins with this letter. It sounds really simple, but it turns out to be a lot of fun. You hear some crazy words and your kids will be amusingly competitive. The point is, don't stress if great conversations don't happen the first time you sit down at the table; it does take time.

Communicating with Other Parents

Now that your son is older, you probably do not have as much contact with other parents. It is still important to try to keep the lines of communication open. Your son will not be very helpful in this pursuit.

Beyond Play Dates

Talking to other parents will aid you in so many ways. It is a great way to find out what is going on in your son's life. You may call other parents for a variety of reasons, including:

- To confirm plans
- To discuss how school is going
- To talk about problems between your teens
- To help minimize manipulation

Talking about Trouble

There may be times when you need to talk to other parents about unpleasant issues. Whether you are calling about problems your son is having with their child or something their child is doing, being nervous is normal.

E Fact

If your son knows you talk with other parents, you reap the benefits. While outwardly he may tell you how it will ruin his reputation, it makes him be honest with you. He knows if he tries to hide something, his cover may be completely blown.

When talking to other parents, you should always tell them who you are and why you are calling. Explain the facts or ask your questions. Always be respectful. Even if you are really upset and know the facts without a doubt, being upset or loud will not help your situation.

Sometimes you will get the information you want and have a very productive conversation. However, the other parent may shut you down and refuse to talk to you. You cannot force others to talk to you. If you need to, you can ask for outside help. School counselors are good third parties you can appeal to for help.

Family Matters

You may be convinced that your teenaged son needs you less as he grows older. While this is true to a certain extent, he also needs you more, just in a different way than he did when he was five years old. Your work as a parent is not done, and your role is still very important.

 Fact

Leave your son love notes. They don't have to be mushy, but put a sticky note on his mirror or in his lunch that says, "Good luck on your test!" Maybe he is having a rough week. Stick a note in his backpack that says, "I'm thinking of you today."

Why Your Son Still Needs You

As tempting as it can be to withdraw from your son's life as he grows older and seemingly less interested in anything you have to say, he still needs you. While some of his teen years are spent learning how to be self-sufficient and laying the foundation for life on his own, he's not ready just yet. He needs to have firm boundaries and to know you are always there for him.

Try to remember the idea of "teachable moments," often discussed in the context of parenting small children. When children ask a question, it is a particularly brilliant opportunity to teach them something about what they are asking. Your teen son will occasionally still ask such questions. When he does, be ready to teach him at this golden opportunity. He may also ask questions indirectly, so sometimes you need to step up and offer your help, even without being asked.

 Alert

Be sure to ask your son questions. This is an easy way to show you are paying attention to him and care what he has to say. "How was your test today?" "What would you like for dinner tomorrow?" Be sure to pay attention to the answers!

Ways to Stay Connected

As your son pulls away, separating himself from you, you may feel left out. It is your responsibility to pull him in and be a part of his life. This does not need to painful. There are many ways to stay in touch with your son and to be a part of his life.

Find out what interests him and jump in. If he is a part of a sports or academic team, you have an easy way to be with him. Simply begin attending his events. He may say he doesn't want you there, but secretly he's pleased you care. It also gives you a chance to see the people he spends a good part of his time with every day.

If the two of you have a mutual interest, take advantage of it! Does he like golf? Take him to the driving range. Maybe he likes music. Go with him to a concert; even though this may not seem like a lot of fun, you might be surprised. Even if you don't have fun listening to the music, being with your son is a reward in itself. Other ways to spend time with your son include:

- Causes he holds near and dear
- Clubs and groups
- Movies
- Civic meetings

Sharing interests can help you forge a bond with your son as an adult. Your role as parent is defined, but he needs to know that you are capable of viewing him as more than a very tall kindergartner.

Chapter 4

Effective
Discipline Techniques

Discipline means many different things to many different parents. The end goal of discipline is typically the same for all parents—to create some order in the chaotic lives of their children and family. Firmly established and correctly applied, discipline can help your son take control of his own life at home and at school. It will give him an idea of cause and effect, and he can use his self-discipline to solve problems in his life.

Defining Discipline

Discipline is defined as a system of rules that apply to behavior. This is very different from what most people believe or think when they hear the word "discipline." Many parents would think of punishment, physical or not. This is where many parents get into problems with discipline. The goal of discipline is to teach your son how to behave properly in society.

Discipline as He Gets Older

When your son was a young boy, discipline meant you taught him some basics of behavior. You taught him to be safe. You taught him to stay alive. These laid the foundation for what he needed to know. He learned to look both ways before crossing the street because if he didn't there was a consequence, either from traffic or his parents. He learned that if he crossed a stated barrier, he would pay the stated price.

 Fact

Avoid changing your mind after the fact. Going easy on your son or changing the rules midstream will only allow him to believe he rules the roost. This shows him he can wheedle his way out of things by asking nicely or begging.

As your son matures, the focus of discipline shifts. It's no longer about these basics; hopefully they have already been mastered. It is about learning to grow and mature on his own in a structured environment. Your job as his parent is to devise that structured environment and select consequences that reinforce the objective or lesson.

Changing Your Attitude

It's no surprise that your son is growing up. He is changing not only physically, but emotionally as well. This can be hard for many parents to accept. One of the most common mistakes parents of teenagers make is to continue to treat their teen the way they treated him as a young boy. The concept of discipline is one of the things that must change with adolescence.

 *Essential*

You must give your son responsibility. You simply can't wait until he turns eighteen and shove him into a cold, cruel world. Your job is to slowly groom your son to be ready. Give him the factual information and the thinking skills he needs.

Now that your son is older, you need to adapt your parenting skills to fit him personally. It means that as a parent you may need to learn to do things differently. For example, you may have an opinion on a decision your son makes. Guess what? It's time you learned to wait for him to ask your opinion rather than freely giving it.

This allows your son to look at a problem and define it. Then it becomes his job to try to find a solution. These are the problem-solving skills that will help him make his life easier as he continues to mature. You need to shift from primary caretaker to lifeguard, only stepping in when his life is in danger, literally or figuratively.

This shift will likely change many of the ways you parent. It may mean you incorporate his ideas into how his life is structured on a daily basis. You may let him have more freedom with every year or milestone, and the disciplinary methods you use will likely change as well.

Setting Boundaries

Everyone needs rules and boundaries. Imagine what driving down a busy street would be like without the rules we have in place. Your son also requires those rules, even if he complains and gripes about them.

Why He Needs Boundaries

Even the most well-behaved, most well-intentioned kid needs boundaries. Boundaries are like safety nets: they define exactly how far children can go without causing or getting into trouble. Teenagers will test the boundaries to see for themselves what will happen if they step over them. They will try to identify weak boundaries to give themselves more freedom. Sometimes your son will bounce up against a boundary only to find out what the consequences are for that infraction.

 Fact

Boys can be overwhelmed and act on instinct. Your son may think with his body and not his brain. To help him realize this and deal with it, gently point it out when you see it and ask him to feel what he is feeling.

The tough part for you is deciding where you need to set the boundaries. They will obviously change as your son learns and grows. They may also change as he stumbles and makes poor choices. The rules and boundaries need to be in place up front.

Present a United Front

Everyone in your home should present a united front when it comes to discipline. This is not something to decide on the fly. You should sit down privately with your spouse and discuss your beliefs about discipline. Then decide what consequences and tactics you will use and how they will be enforced.

 *Essential*

All boys will test the waters, so to speak. This testing can be scary for parents. Remember to relax and take deep breaths, stepping in only when absolutely needed. You won't be there all the time, and he has to learn to make decisions for himself.

A plan makes discipline easier to administer. When an infraction occurs, everyone, including your son, should know what the consequences will be and how the issue will be addressed. A united front also shows your son that coming to either of you separately will not affect the outcome—you stand together.

Setting Boundaries

Whether you call them rules or boundaries, the goal is the same—to elicit a specific response from your son. It is important that you choose the boundaries for your son as an individual. You should know him best and know where his strengths and weaknesses lie.

Keep the following points in mind when you set boundaries, and keep in mind that some may have less to do with your son and more with you:

- Consistency; parents need to be a team in discipline.
- Be sure what you are asking of your son is reasonable.
- Consequences should be fair and logical.
- Remember your son can only respond within his own capabilities.

As teens push the boundaries, it is important for parents to push back. Boundaries are essential to letting your son recognize that there are limits to what he can do.

How to Fight

The naked truth is that at some point you will probably argue with your son. The argument may be over something big or something small. In the end, you may not even remember what you were arguing about, though you remember fighting.

The Rules of Arguments

Most parents understand that arguments are inevitable. How soon they happen, how often they happen, and how long they last are completely different for everyone. While you can't control some arguments, others are completely within your control. By learning to minimize arguments ahead of time, you can spare you and your son some heartache.

Fact

> Don't pick fights. Sometimes it's easy to do if you've had a rotten day or your son is doing something that annoys you. Remember that you are the adult in this situation and you have to be the one to step back.

It is best to fight fairly. Have rules for both you and your son to follow when you fight. The following is a nice starter list of rules, but be sure to add to it as you need to for your unique family situation.

- Be respectful
- Do not yell
- Do not engage in name-calling
- No physical violence is permitted
- Use active listening skills
- Keep discussions on topic
- Don't bring up the past
- Be open; neither of you can read minds
- Use "I" statements to own your feelings and thoughts
- _____
- _____
- _____
- _____
- _____

Adhering to these rules can help protect both you and your son from saying things you don't mean and making the problem worse.

Minimize Arguments

While you cannot avoid all conflict, there are things that you can do to help minimize it. The family unit has to agree upon it together in order for it to work.

 **Essential**

> The punishment should always fit the crime. You need to remember that the consequences are logical or natural and should be appropriate for the infraction. When this doesn't happen, your son rarely learns the lesson.

The first step is to call a family meeting. At this meeting, work hard to come up with a list of possible, realistic infractions. Then work together as a family to come up with a list of consequences for each infraction.

Writing the rules down before a conflict arises allows everyone a chance to participate in the decision-making and shows your son you care about his thoughts and feelings. It also allows everyone to decide on the consequences while there is no conflict. This means that people are less likely to be angry and the decisions are likely to be more sound. Finally, writing rules down in advance also gives everyone ownership of the rules, making it more likely that your children will follow them, or if they break them, more likely to willingly accept responsibility and the consequences.

Individualized Discipline

Not every form of discipline will work for every child. For example, if your son doesn't like to watch television, removing the ability to watch television isn't going to bother him. The same goes for the boy who likes to be alone in his room; it is not a punishment to be sent to his room. Keep the child in mind when deciding the consequences. If your kids cry foul, simply explain that everyone needs an individualized plan for consequences.

Natural or Logical Consequences

Natural consequences are those that follow a natural progression. They are reactions that are appropriate for the crime. They logically follow a mistake.

Natural Consequences

Natural consequences happen because of an action. These consequences tend to be ones that you as a parent can't control. While they may be immediate, they can also be harmful. An example might be putting your hand on a hot stove: doing so has a tangible consequence, and while you can try to prevent your son from touching the stove in the first place, the consequences are out of your control once he puts his hand on it. As a parent, you strive to spare your son the most painful consequences. There are times when your son will have to learn for himself, but sometimes there are ways to get the point across without putting him in danger.

Using natural consequences is not always possible because such consequences are not always immediate or appropriate. If your son chose to have sex without a condom, he may or may not get someone pregnant, or pass on or contract a sexually transmitted infection, but the consequences or lack thereof don't make the action appropriate. Such situations are not a time to depend on natural consequences because of the danger he is in.

Ⓔ *Essential*

Your goals must be well defined. If you say your son's grades have to improve, define what that means. You might require a GPA no lower than a 3.0 with no single grade below a C every semester.

Logical Consequences

Logical consequences are thought through before they are applied. They usually have something to do with the problem. Let's say your son doesn't write down his homework, so he can't remember what it was that he was supposed to do. As a result, his homework doesn't get done or is done improperly. He then earns a poor grade for that homework assignment. The consequence—a bad grade—follows a logical progression.

When setting up the consequences, keep in mind that your goal should be for the consequence to send a message. That message should be related to the infraction. Let's say your son misses his curfew. He comes in about thirty minutes late. Without screaming or yelling, you already have the consequences in place—he loses thirty minutes off of his next venture. He knows it, and you know it. The next time he goes out he is forced to remember why it is he needs to come home earlier than usual.

The Follow-Through

Isn't the follow-through always the hardest part of everything? The problem is that the follow-through is everything when it comes to discipline. Hence, it is also one of the biggest problems that parents have when working on discipline.

The Difficulties of the Follow-Through

Follow-through sends the message that you are paying attention and that you mean business. It tells your son you love him enough to ensure he learns a lesson, even if it is hard.

 Fact

If your son spends time at your home and at another home, as in the case of divorced parents, it may be more difficult for punishments to happen. Talk together as co-parents to decide how punishments will be handled so that you can all present a united front, even within different households.

But there are many barriers to follow-through. The first barrier is likely you. You may have other things on your mind, or have forgotten what you had previously said the consequence would be for a specific behavior. Perhaps you've made a threat that wasn't reasonable or possible. This means that you also won't follow through or will only partially follow through.

The second barrier to follow-through will be your son. Guess what? It should come as no surprise if he doesn't really want to remind you what his punishment is supposed to be. His job is going to be to distract you or to persuade you not to follow through. He is motivated to escape the consequences.

Ensuring You Follow-Through

So what can a parent do to ensure that follow-through happens? The first step is to be sure you write down everything you agree to with your son. This can be a piece of paper or a computer file, but you should keep it in a place where everyone can see it. This also serves as a reminder to your son about not breaking the rules. The consequences are prearranged and agreed upon.

While having the list handy should help you remember to follow through, the barriers are out there, and sometimes it's easier and more comfortable to allow them to defeat you. If your issue is laziness, you need to take a long look at your goals as a parent of your child. If your issue is disorganization, you need to find a place to store this document so that it is handy. If your issue is simple forgetfulness, actually write down the steps for how you want the discussion and issuance of the consequence to go.

Let Him Be the Judge

Your son will have a good idea what punishment is by the time he is in his mid-teens. It is time to start enlisting his help in the matter of his discipline. This can help him develop a sense of responsibility over his behavior.

Teen Attitudes Toward Consequences

When people are given the chance, it's natural human instinct to try to avoid consequences. As a teen, sometimes the pull to do the wrong thing prevails or your son simply may not stop to think about the consequences. This is part of how teens think, whether parents like it or not.

 Fact

When asked what was the most severe form of punishment a teen could receive, 26 percent of the teens in intact families and 44 percent of the teens in stepfamilies said that grounding was the most severe punishment.

Consequences are meant as deterrents. They are designed to help your son think twice—or more, if necessary—before acting. Your son is not going to smile and say, "Thanks!" The thanks comes in knowing you are doing the right thing as a parent. Eventually, your son will realize the value of the consequences. Don't waver because of a few stomps, tears, or other theatrics.

Enlist Your Son's Help

Your biggest ally in helping to find the appropriate consequences or punishment will be none other than your son himself. Don't shy away from asking for his help. By asking for his help, you are saying you value his judgment and opinions. You are also telling him that you trust him to take ownership of the issues at hand.

Essential

While it is tempting to constantly remind your son of the negative impact a certain action or behavior will have on his life, it's probably not the best policy. A study in *Behavior Modification* suggests it is important not only to avoid this behavior, but also to involve your son in his own discipline.

By having your son help you choose the punishments for certain transgressions, you also get him to acknowledge the behaviors as inappropriate. He may need your guidance in choosing appropriate responses to certain behaviors. This is also a part of his growing and learning, which should be a joint effort. You should always try to share the responsibility, but realize that as the parent, you are the last word in arguments.

Punishing Yourself

One of the problems with punishing your son is that sometimes you end up inadvertently punishing yourself. This need not be a problem if you are aware of this possibility. There are two ways to punish yourself when punishing your son.

It's Not Your Fault

When you have to punish your son, remember that he made a choice that deserved a prearranged punishment. He knew going in that his decision might lead to the consequence. He made the decision knowing the consequence was not only possible but probable.

 **Alert**

Whatever you say should be something that you are willing to do. Don't threaten him with things that are obviously not going to happen, and avoid statements like "You're grounded until you're eighteen!"

Your son forced your hand by making a bad decision. Despite any complaints on his part, you are doing exactly what is necessary to be a good parent. Don't doubt yourself. You are sticking to the original plan and agreement. Do not waver.

How Does the Punishment Affect You?

Another way to punish yourself is to make bad judgments about the consequence. This will mean different things to different parents. In any case, whatever the consequence, you should not suffer physically, emotionally, or monetarily. Only you can decide what punishments would have acceptable consequences for you.

E Essential

Admit when you are wrong. While it can be difficult to be wrong in front of your children, it is an important character-building lesson. It will teach your children that adults make mistakes and also take responsibility for those mistakes.

If you and your son are having difficulties spending time in the same room together, it would be a punishment to ground your son to the house for a very long period of time. It would also most likely be overkill. This is why consequences are best laid out ahead of time and not in the heat of anger.

Chapter 5

Your Son's Self-Esteem

How your son feels about himself is probably one of the most important topics to discuss because it will affect—positively or negatively—everything he does. As a parent, you can nurture positive self-esteem in your teenage son, but other influences outside your control also affect him. Your son's self-esteem during his adolescent years will stay with him and have an impact on the man he becomes. What you can do as a parent to nurture an appropriate self-esteem is also important and something that he will live with for the rest of his life.

What Is Self-Esteem?

Self-esteem is a collection of thoughts or feelings we hold about ourselves. These feelings begin to develop at an early age and influence nearly everything in our lives.

Helping Develop a Good Self-Esteem

Children with a healthy self-esteem are more adaptable. They tend to be happier and better adjusted. Parents play a big part in developing healthy self-esteem in their children. One of the best things you can do is to be a good role model. If you have a negative self-esteem, you risk passing it along to your son. If he sees you constantly saying negative things about yourself or being unrealistic about your abilities and limitations, he will adopt these feelings about himself. But if you exhibit signs of a positive self-esteem, your son will learn those habits from you. Parents with a high self-esteem tend to be more affectionate and supportive and set firmer guidelines for their son's behavior.

When dealing with your son's difficult situations, including failures, be sure to focus on the efforts your son makes. Be sure to tell him that you're proud of him for trying. It is important to be realistic. Do not focus on the outcomes.

 *Essential*

By giving your child physical attention like hugs and kisses, you can help raise his self-esteem by letting him know you value him. Be sure to do so in a location and in a way that is acceptable to your son.

Negative Self-Esteem

Signs that your son has a negative self-esteem include a negative outlook on just about everything. He may have a low tolerance for frustration and be reluctant to try new things for fear of failure. If you find your son constantly being critical of himself, you should seek the help of a qualified counselor to help get things on the right track. Left unchecked, a low self-esteem can lead to depression and other problems.

That said, it's not abnormal for your son to experience short periods of being down in the dumps. If your son seems to be in a funk and you aren't sure if it's a low self-esteem or just a bad couple of weeks, talk to him. He might be able to quickly allay your fears and verbalize that he is simply a bit down over something very specific. Be more worried if he has a general state of depression and can't seem to break out of the cycle.

Too Much of a Good Thing?

Narcissism is on the rise, according to W. Keith Campbell, a psychology professor at the University of Georgia. Having too much self-esteem can lead your son into trouble. Narcissistic personalities are more likely to have failures in relationships and tend to lack empathy and react poorly to criticism.

E *Fact*

When parents are less involved, teens' peer relationships become overly important to them. The negative pressure can increase, which may lead to your son experimenting with or abusing drugs and alcohol.

While it is important for your son to realize that he has special talents and dreams, learning to recognize these same qualities in others is a crucial social skill. He must also learn that everyone fails at something. You simply can't expect to be perfect in all you do. Learning that lesson early is usually easier than when you're away from home and lack the safety net of your parents.

Finding the Good

There are days when your son will get on your nerves. His grades may be low, and maybe he's got a rude temper to boot. It doesn't matter. Your job is to always find the good in him.

Reward Him for Good Behavior

Many schools have learned that by catching kids being good, they have a chance to reward good behavior, which is more meaningful to a teen than punishment for bad behavior. This is a skill parents need to master.

E Essential

Delegating responsibilities to your teen son sends the message that you have faith in his ability to complete a task well. Offer him the skills he needs, but in the end, recognize that he needs to be left alone to complete the task so that he can, alone, bask in the glory of a job well done.

Many teens naturally excel at something. It might be at school or perhaps in sports. Look beyond grades and game wins. It is important to say, "Hey, it was great that you helped your teammate make the goal, and even though you didn't get credit, I noticed you helped him. Way to go!"

Reward your son around the house for being helpful, even if he only does a few little things. You might praise him for taking his clothes to his room, for instance. Though at first they may believe you are being sarcastic, keep it up and find something to compliment. The rules to this are only that it has to be truthful and it has to be good.

Having Trouble Finding the Good?

If you are having a problem finding good things about your son, you need to stop and take inventory. Is it really that he is not doing good things at all? Ever? Or is it simply that you are not witnessing good things?

Ⓔ Question

How can I help my son have a good body image?
While boys are less likely than girls to suffer from eating disorders, it does happen. Try to avoid saying negative things about your own weight and eating habits.

If it is simply a matter of you not being around to see your son do good things, find a way to change your schedule to put yourself in a situation to see him do something appropriate. You really do need to go out of your way to say "Good job!"

If you really think your son is not doing enough good things, you need to change that situation. This is true even if it means you orchestrate events to help him do something positive. It might be something as simple as doing his homework or taking his dishes to the sink after dinner. Starting small is the only way; from there your son will hopefully get a clue and start doing it on his own. Once he has a taste of praise he might find he likes it.

Watching Criticism

It is easy to let words slip that are harmful to your son's self-esteem. You might be focused more on the outcome than on the effort, or maybe you're angry over something that has happened, like a poor grade on his report card. Criticism is necessary, but it hurts. There are ways for you to make your point without hurting your son's self-esteem.

Criticism Can Be Poison

Criticism is typically a negative force both on the surface and below. When you criticize inappropriately, you actually tear down your son's self-esteem. It cuts deeply for your son because of his trust and love for you, more than do the hurtful words of others.

There is a time and a place for positive, constructive criticism. The difference is that in constructive criticism you are trying to build your son up, not tear him down.

Build up the potential and accentuate the positive: "You are really a very smart kid, I know you can do better on your exam. Maybe a bit more preparation will help you next time." Don't focus on the negative: "You are so stupid, you can't even pass a silly English test."

Criticism can be verbal, but you can also convey your criticism through your attitude toward him, such as through excessive punishments to prove a point or teach a lesson. Every negative act you take toward your son is potentially harmful. Be careful and think about every word that comes out of your mouth.

Your home needs to be a safe place, a place that is free of hurtful statements and criticism. This can be hard to do. If you find that you say something to your child that is harmful or hurtful, apologize. Be real and explain what happened when you apologize. Show your son that mistakes happen and negative things are sometimes said, but that if you honestly made a mistake you can ask for and hopefully receive forgiveness.

Ⓔ *Essential*

As he pushes the boundaries, your son will push your buttons. Be sure you have an exit strategy; take a timeout before dealing out your punishment or imparting your wise words. Your son can learn to handle his anger by watching you.

Find Positive Ways to Criticize

Just because you need to be wary of what you say or do near your son doesn't mean that he never needs to be redirected or punished. You simply need to do it in a way that helps him grow rather than tears him down. Again, setting a good example is the best way to teach him.

Ⓔ *Essential*

If you don't do your homework, you get a bad grade. This lesson is one that is hard to learn when you're falling on your face. You cannot save your son from these consequences. They have to be learned, hopefully only one time.

Set your son up with situations that allow him to grow and learn. You can use role-playing, but also show him how to mend broken fences in real life. Positive criticism is a way to show him that you care and that while he has made mistakes, there is a lesson to be learned to help prevent him from making more mistakes. Remind him that failures aren't always a bad thing, and that every lesson in life can be a positive one if turned around and learned from.

Bullying

Bullying is bad news. Bullying can lead to low self-esteem in your son. About 30 percent of teens say that they have been the subject of bullying, have been a bully, or both, according to the National Youth Violence Prevention Resource Center.

How Bullies Work

Bullies are mean and disrespectful of others, and they can be male or female. They use inappropriate behavior to try to feel powerful. In the end, bullying is all about control. The bully uses the bad behavior as a way to manipulate others so that he feels like he has power over others. A bully usually has normal to high levels of self-esteem. There are two main types of bullies, those who are overt—which are the ones we tend to think about most often—and those who are covert. Covert bullies are a bit more hidden but every bit as dangerous.

 Fact

There are resources to help you and your son learn how to cope with violence and not be a part of it. The National Youth Violence Prevention Resource Center has some great resources for parents at *http://safeyouth.org*.

A bully may have many tactics in his arsenal. A bully may be physical and may resort to violence in the form of hitting, kicking, pinching, biting, or any other physical harm. A bully can also use the threat of physical harm to intimidate someone.

Bullying can also involve sexual, religious, and racial slurs. Bullies tell inappropriate jokes on purpose, with the intent to cause harm or discomfort. Bullying can involve unwanted physical contact or inappropriate gestures.

Emotional bullying is more common in girls but can be found in boys as well. It is the subtle ignoring of people, the picking someone last in line at gym class—something everyone dreads, including your son. Spreading rumors about someone is also a form of bullying.

Bullies are found everywhere. Though the societal perception is that a bully is from the schoolyard, you can also find bullies at the bus stop, on the playground, and at any social event where you find kids. It is part of your job as a parent to teach your son about bullying. Teach him what the characteristics of bullies are, then teach him appropriate ways to deal with bullies. You should work hard to show him the proper channels to work within if he feels he is being abused by a bully.

 *Alert*

Cyber-bullying is when threatening or defamatory e-mails, instant messages, blog posts, or even cell-phone messages are used to abuse someone. Cyber-bullying is harmful because it hits your teen where he would normally feel safe—at home.

Is Your Son Being Bullied?

The good news is that bullying tends to be found more with younger teens than older teens, though this is not written in stone. You can see the toll bullying takes on your son. Bullying can lead your son to avoid previously fun situations like school or sports. You may find that he invents mysterious illnesses to avoid locations where he comes in contact with the bully. Your son may also begin to exhibit signs of depression, unexplained injuries like bruising, and inexplicably lost items, including lunch money. He may wait to use the bathroom at home to avoid bullies or try to carry a knife or a gun to protect himself.

 **E-Fact**

It is important to remember that boys with low self-esteem are not always depressed or quiet. In fact, sometimes it is quite the opposite. You may find that a child with low self-esteem is actually loud, rude, aggressive, and has poor impulse control.

Parents cannot rely on the school system to tell them about bullying that goes on at school. Sometimes bullies have the school officials charmed into believing that they are really great kids or simply misunderstood. If you suspect bullying, you should notify the school. Remember that persistence is very important when dealing with bullies. Your son's school may already be aware of the bully. Then you can talk to your son about how to handle the bully. The following guidelines may help your son learn to deal with bullying:

- Avoid places where bully hangs out whenever possible.
- Act confident.
- Walk away if possible.
- Ignore what you can.
- Use humor.
- Tell a responsible adult, such as a teacher.
- Occasionally, agree with the bully and let it go.

If your son is being bullied, there are a number of things that you can do to help him. It is important that you help him build a strong peer group and bolster his confidence by reminding him that he is a good kid, that he does things well, and that he cannot be responsible for what other kids say or do. When appropriate, show him how to stand up to a bully, assuming that your son's safety is not an issue. Tell him to say, firmly, "I don't like it when you do that, so stop." A bully will always seek out someone who is "weaker" than he is to pick on. A bully will rarely target someone who has a large number of friends or high self-esteem. If bullying is affecting your son's self-esteem, it is time to seek professional help.

Is Your Son a Bully?

While you may be tempted to ignore behavior that is bully-like in your son, it is important to know the facts. Bullies are more likely to shoplift, vandalize, cut school, and abuse drugs and alcohol. One study showed that a bully is four times more likely to be arrested, with 60 percent of bullies having at least one conviction by the time they are twenty-four years old. Some signs that your son may be predisposed to being a bully include:

- Quickness to anger
- Cocky or arrogant behavior
- Low tolerance for frustration
- Difficulty accepting authority
- Impulsive behavior
- Little empathy for others

If you think your son has an issue with bullying, you need to help him. Begin by talking to him about behaviors that are inappropriate. Explain what the consequences will be for behavior you deem to be bullying. These punishments should be nonviolent and nonphysical. Try to spend more time with your son so that you can show him proper behavior. You can also request support from his school. If these steps don't seem to make an improvement, be sure to seek professional support.

 Fact

While teens will tell you they really dislike your presence, research shows that it really does benefit them. In the end they wind up being grateful that you cared, because that is what parental involvement really means.

Fear of Failure

Failure is a fact of life. It is not a pleasant fact, but it is a fact. Everyone will have to deal with some form of failure in life. By learning to cope with it, your child can gain confidence and learn resilience.

Avoiding Failure

The fact that failure is unavoidable doesn't make it any more pleasant to encounter. Some teenagers are more sensitive to making mistakes than others. Your son may make a few huge mistakes or a series of little ones over the course of his adolescence. Each of these mistakes is a lesson in the making. So, no matter how hard he tries, he will encounter failure, which is not a bad thing.

What can be detrimental is if parents try to fix his pain. You cannot fix his problems, or he will not have learned the lesson. If you constantly save him, you aren't really helping your son. He will eventually make the same mistakes and have to recover when he may not have the safety net of your home and constant attention.

While your teen may be determined to avoid failure, it is important to remind him that this is not the ideal. Avoiding failure will not help your son. It is how he learns to deal with failure and turn it around that will help him gain the knowledge that is required to grow to adulthood.

Why Failure Is Good

One of the hard lessons your teenaged son needs to learn is how to recover from adversity. This means that he will have to take some hard knocks as he grows, usually in his teen years. Your job as a parent is to stand by and provide loose boundaries—but not to save him.

 *Alert*

Teen depression is tied to your son's self-esteem in many ways. Depression is also a risk factor for teen suicide, which is more common in young men than in young women, as is low self-esteem.

It is hard as a parent to sit and watch your son lose something like a school election or a big game. But ultimately he will be stronger for this if you allow him to have these feelings.

If you save him, you prevent him from learning the lesson he needed to learn from this failure.

Your job while he is learning and growing is to show him that you will always be there for him. You need to show him that you have faith in him and that you trust him to make decisions for himself. By backing off and letting him deal with the situation, you are ultimately saying you trust his ability to deal with the problem. That can, in the end, be a huge boost in confidence, no matter how painful it is for you in the moment.

Fear of Success

Sometimes teenagers do not live up to their full potential. This is an unfortunate fact. It is painful for all involved and certainly hard to watch, particularly when it is your son.

Signs Your Son Is Afraid of Success

Perhaps you are not sure what you're looking for, but there is something that is just not quite right with your son. Do his grades not reflect what his test scores tell you they should be? Perhaps he has a secret passion he's not showing in school—that he loves to write poetry or play the violin—and yet is barely passing English class and refuses to join the orchestra.

He may be worried that getting good grades isn't cool, or perhaps he's afraid his friends will ditch him if he shows his true talents or brains. That is really a problem when you are trying to convince him otherwise. Sometimes your son wants to hide because of the special treatment that would call attention to him. He may be fearful that if he were to attempt to break out of his comfort zone and "go for it," he might actually fail.

Overcoming the Fear of Success

If you can get to the heart of why your son has a fear of doing well, you might have an easier time trying to solve this puzzle. Unfortunately, he may not even be able to give you a truthful answer, even if he wanted to do so. It is always easier to just stay where you are than to overcome inertia and change.

Sometimes using a rewards system can work well. Offer to send him to a special course that feeds into his talents or offer him some guitar lessons, if he meets certain criteria. The trick is to be realistic. You can't say that he has to bring his failing grades up to be straight A's. You might set a goal for something along the lines of a 3.0 each semester with no failures. That gives your son some wiggle room. He might get a D in math, but he may also bring up the rest of his grades to strive for that 3.0. Find a bargain that works well for him and remind him that later on, school is much different.

E Essential

Remember that even if he doesn't succeed in school, or he isn't the captain of the football team or even on the team, your son does have something that he is good at. Your job is to find out what that something is and to praise him for it.

College is usually a great place for people who have been suffering from a fear of success in high school. College is a time to reinvent yourself and not worry about old stereotypes. It is a chance for your son to start fresh and make a new life for himself. The problem is that many times, if your son has been underperforming in high school, college can be difficult to get into or to get financial aid or scholarships for, so it can be a double-edged sword.

Pressure to Be Perfect

The pressure to be the perfect kid is widespread. It winds up eating some students alive. They feel the pressure to perform at school, at home, and in sports.

The Pressure to Succeed

Because teens today face a lot of pressure, they may feel that there is only one right way. Your son may feel that football is the only sport or that a specific college is the only one available. Once he has his sights on something, he may turn around and press himself really hard to make that dream a reality.

Seeing a dream and going for it may not seem like a big deal. The problem comes in when your son becomes obsessed with a particular dream or goal to the point of excluding all other options. This is when it becomes unhealthy.

Your son may actually exhibit physical symptoms of stress. This can include headaches, stomach problems, and sleep disturbances. The obsessions are unhealthy when they bring him to the point of these physical manifestations.

How to Contain the Pressure

Parents are programmed to tell their children to do well. Sometimes it works, and sometimes it doesn't. One of the things parents often forget to teach kids is that they do not expect perfection.

Talk to your son and explain what your expectations really are for him. Do you expect him to be perfect? What does he think the consequences are of "failing" to be perfect? You may find that he is worried that your love is conditional on his success. Be sure to reassure him that you love him for who he is and not what he does.

One of the most important lessons you can teach your son is how to fail gracefully. This means that he learns to gather up the pieces and figure out what to do next. He needs to learn to take the lesson from his mistake and move on with a new idea or path for his goal. This will help lead him to the path of self-reliance and resilience.

Chapter 6

Your Son's Self-Image

Looking in the mirror and liking what you see is an important part of life and of growing up. The problem is that it is possible for this image to become distorted. When this happens, it throws your son's life off kilter. As his parent, you can help him maintain an accurate image and show him how to avoid the pitfalls of self-image.

Body Image

Body image is how your son views his physical appearance. Puberty will alter his face, his body type, even his voice. This can make establishing positive body image a difficult job.

Thin Is In

Thin is very in, even with boys. Your son may see being thin as a way to achieve popularity, favor with his crush, and material wealth. The media perpetuates this image. Occasionally your son may be exposed to the jolly fat friend on television, but the main character is always the thin, sexy man.

It is important that you set the stage with your son to help him process all of the images and information that he is bombarded with, not only on television but also in magazines and music videos. He needs to understand that his body is something that he should take care of and treat well. This means proper nutrition, exercise, and care.

 Alert

While eating disorders are more common in girls, boys are also susceptible to them. This is usually as a result of poor body image. Look for signs of disordered eating, and talk to your son's health care practitioner if you are concerned.

Taking Care of His Body

Parents teach their children how to care for their bodies from a young age. At first, this involves simple tasks like bathing and getting rid of diapers. Consciously or unconsciously, parents also show their children how best to select fuel for their bodies by choosing certain foods. Add exercise to the mix and your son has a solid foundation in caring for his greatest asset—his body, the vehicle in which he will live the rest of his life.

Helping your son define his physical goals can also help him see he really is in control of his body. If your son is constantly making disparaging remarks about his body, or you find him undertaking extreme diets, taking weight-loss medications, or exercising overzealously, it is time to see your health care practitioner for advice.

Appearance and Cleanliness

Dirt and mud are two words often associated with boys. Boys often get a bad rap for being messy and smelly—but do they deserve it?

Skin and Hair

Your son's skin may take a nosedive once puberty hits. All of a sudden, he may have to deal with unsightly, acne-riddled skin. Introduce him to over-the-counter facial cleansers and medications to help clear problem acne. Talk to your health care provider about acne that doesn't respond well to topical treatments.

 Fact

Accutane is a powerful anti-acne medication for severe acne. Only a doctor can prescribe it. Since there are risks associated with it, you will also have to have your son's blood checked while he takes Accutane. Visit the American Academy of Dermatology at *www.aad.org* for more information.

Your son's hair has been in your control for years. Giving up the control of his hairstyle may or may not be easy for you, but it is essential to your son that you do so.

If, as he begins to get older, he is still letting you take charge of the haircuts, start asking your son about his likes and dislikes. This can help to ease the transition for both of you, though it won't stop him from coming home one day and announcing he wants a mohawk. A word of warning: Unlike body-piercing parlors, hair salons don't require parents to be there.

Your son may develop an interest in hair-care products that go beyond shampoo and conditioner. Many young men use other products to enhance curl or hold their hairstyle in place. This is perfectly normal.

Hygiene

Good hygiene is a must. You may find that adolescent boys sometimes aren't as good at the daily shower as others. Be sure to talk to your son about taking a regular shower or bath. Let him choose which he prefers. Explain that there are certain times when he really should shower, such as after working out or playing sports.

 Fact

Flossing is an important topic even for teens. While parents may simply be relieved that they can get their son to brush his teeth, teaching him the importance of flossing now can help him incorporate this into his daily regimen more easily.

If you have a problem convincing your son to bathe or shower, there are some strategies to help. First of all, be sure to praise him whenever he showers on his own. Compliment him honestly any chance you get on his cleanliness. Notice if he goes out of his way to look or smell nice. This can help him have positive associations with cleanliness. Sometimes allowing him to use a men's cologne when he showers also helps.

Products to Aid in Cleanliness

Deodorant is a must. Teaching your son to get in the habit of wearing it should start early. Be sure to emphasize that everyone has body odor and that it is normal. This will help him not feel like you think he smells, even if it is true. Letting him choose his own deodorant may be helpful. There are special products marketed toward teens for hygiene purposes. They may be a bit more expensive, but if your son actually uses the products, it may be worth the cost.

When your son is ready to start shaving, help him pick products to protect his skin. He may have sensitive skin and frequent shaving might make his skin sore. Acne can be an issue when shaving, so be sure to stay on top of acne with cleanliness and treatment.

Good old-fashioned soap and water will take care of most of what ails him, though a few nice products may encourage him to take better care of himself. For this alone, the extra price is probably worth it.

Trends and Designer Clothes

Remember when it was easy to dress your son? You had five or six solid-colored T-shirts and several pairs of jeans, with an occasional nice outfit thrown in for good measure. Those days are long gone. What your son wears now will play a large part in determining how he feels about himself. Give him some freedom. Letting him pick out and buy his own clothes helps teach him how to care for himself and how to fit into society.

The Basics of Clothing

What your son wears will help him identify himself. Your ability to have any say in what he wears has just about gone out the window. That said, you are still the fashion police.

 Fact

Be very leery of alcohol- or tobacco-related articles of clothing. Your son might insist that they are jokes, but studies have shown that some of these items do seem to be related with the use of the product.

Your son will have certain ideas about what he wants to wear and how he wants to wear it. Schools may have rules about what he wears and how his clothes look on his body, which means he'll save all of his clothing angst for you, after school hours.

Develop some straightforward rules early on and enforce them. Your rules might include the following:

- No clothing that makes reference to drugs or violence is allowed.
- Clothes must be worn as designed: no pants dragging to the knees, no external underwear.
- He must care for his clothes, including washing and mending them.

Fashion Trends

Boys are just as susceptible to fashion trends as their female counterparts. They don't go far in life without seeing something aimed at them from a marketing perspective. You don't have to look any further than big teen clothing retailers like Abercrombie & Fitch and Gap to see that teen fashion is an important part of their marketing strategy.

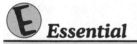 **Essential**

> Some of the most fashionable clothes and shoes can be wildly expensive. Consider sharing your clothing budget with your son so that he can see how far your money has to stretch. Strategize together how you can come up with extra money for other items he wants that the budget doesn't cover.

Remind your son that he is an individual. Help him select clothing that looks good on his body type. Compliment him on his style of dress, and assist him in finding a happy medium between being one of the crowd and finding his own sense of style.

Accessories

Your son may be interested in some minor accessories like hats, sunglasses, jewelry, and belts. These help him define his fashion sense.

More and more boys are getting their ears pierced because it is fashionable. Discuss with him why he wants to do it and how you feel about it. While you must consent for him to get his ears pierced at a shop until he is eighteen, it doesn't mean that he and his friends won't pierce his ears at the next football game or after party. Be clear about what you want and need from your son.

 **E-Fact**

If you are having a problem with your son leaving his clothes everywhere from the bedroom floor to the laundry room floor to the bathroom floor, consider buying more hampers to help him keep the clothes contained.

His Space

Your son will probably love his room. It will be a safe haven for him. His room will be his own space, a place to retreat from the world and just hang out with few pressures. He will decorate it to reflect his personal style, and he will become territorial about sharing it with you or anyone else.

Room Rules

Your son probably craves some privacy in his room. This is understandable, but he has to realize that his space is still a part of your home. This means you get to call the final shots. You should discuss his privacy and the rules surrounding it before it becomes a conflict.

Set the rules up for violations that will allow you to enter the room. Usually these are important problems like:

- Safety issues regarding electricity and fire (inspect sockets and fire detectors)
- Health issues (food, bugs, rodents)
- Issues of security (if his behavior indicates drug use)

Decorating His Space

Try to give your son as much leeway as you can when it comes to fixing up his room. Be sure you go over the budget and the rules with him. One big rule should be that he can't decorate his room in a way that will ultimately destroy the structure should you wish to change it later. Painting, posters, and the like are common means of decorating.

You may find that he is also very interested in entertainment. Music is a great thing for his room, but televisions and computers are not such stellar options. It's easy for him to cloister himself in his room with only a television or computer for company, and parents should be especially wary of letting their children have Internet access without parental supervision.

Essential

When you are looking into paint for your son's room, consider paying a little bit more to get washable paint. This can help the paint last longer and look better longer. Let's face it—kids and non-washable walls aren't a great combination.

Cleaning His Room

As a parent, you must know by now that the room of a teen boy is rarely spotless. And that really is okay. If you are excessively neat, don't hold your son to the same standards.

E Essential

If your son shares living space with a brother, be prepared for some turmoil. See if you can get them to come up with a set of working rules to live by so that your sons appeal to you for parental guidance only in extreme circumstances. This can help your sons learn to negotiate and live with others.

By the time your son is a teen, he is ready to take over the cleaning chores for his living space. At minimum, he should:

- Change the sheets weekly
- Take the garbage out of the room weekly
- Make sure his dirty clothes reach the hamper daily
- Find the sources behind weird and foul odors and eliminate them

Assure your son you really are most interested in guaranteeing that his room is an inhabitable space.

The Physical Nature of Boys

Sports are a great way for your son to stay physically fit, participate with a team, and learn social skills. They are an effective way for him to burn excess energy and boost his confidence.

What Boys Need

Exercise helps your son maintain his weight and grow in strength. It helps him feel better emotionally and physically.

Fact

Physical activity is a great way to boost your son's mood. The release of endorphins during and after exercise is a superb way to keep mild depression in check. It also will help your son feel strong and confident.

Allow your son to pick activities he is interested in. For some boys this is obvious, but others don't seem very interested in sports or physical activity. If you can encourage it, it can be a great way to get your son socially involved and physically active.

Remember that not everyone enjoys group sports. If your son needs the structure of something organized but doesn't like group sports, consider placing him in something that is more individual, such as swimming or cross-country running.

Loves Sports

Your son may love sports. He may excel at particular sport and spend most of his time, on and off season, working toward personal goals within this sport. These goals are a good way for your son to set his own agenda and learn what it takes to get what he wants. Sports can also help your son adapt socially, particularly as he moves from middle to high school.

ⓔ *Essential*

If your son becomes injured playing a sport, be sure you find proper medical care for him. No matter how difficult it may be to sit on the sidelines, it is not worth the risk of permanent injury to play too soon.

However, problems may arise when your son can think of nothing but sports. Try to help your son take interest, even minimally, in other things. Remind him that grades are important, even if he is the star pitcher or quarterback.

Talk to him about his future and how his sport will fit into his life. If he thinks he's going to college on a sports scholarship, gently remind him that the competition is stiff and many colleges look for well-rounded individuals. This may help him find a happy medium between grades and the playing field.

When possible, use your son's love of sports as a common ground. Go with him to his games and become his greatest fan. Having him see you cheering in the sidelines will make his heart swell with pride, even when he claims you are simply embarrassing him.

Hates Sports

Your son might dislike playing sports, and there could be many reasons for his aversion. Perhaps he has a negative association with sports. Maybe he doesn't like the feeling of getting lost in large team. Talk to him to figure out why he isn't interested.

You have to remember that your son's dislike of sports is not a personal reflection of you as a parent. You may have dreamed of the day that you could attend a high school soccer game with your son as a starting goalie, but it might not happen. Being a parent means that you need to learn to let your son decide what is best for him and where his talents lie.

The issue might be finding the right sport for your son. If a group activity isn't his thing, try to find individual sports that he might enjoy. Remind him that being active doesn't have to involve competing against anyone else, and that he can do it just for the love of moving.

 Fact

Cross-training is a great way to help build muscles that might not be as strong as the main ones your son relies on. Take him running or bike riding or consider doing appropriate weight training with him.

You may already know your son has a health issue brewing. If he has issues with his weight, poor nutrition, and lack of exercise, it is imperative that he start moving. First he should visit his health care practitioner for help in starting a plan. From there, work together to stay healthy as a family.

Chapter 7

Building Your
Son's Character

For most people, the image of the man your son is destined to become is one of good character and values. As he progresses through adolescence, you will see your son's value set begin to crystallize. The question then becomes how you as a parent can ensure your son learns what you have to teach him.

Critical Thinking

Making decisions and organizing steps of action based on a logical analysis of the risks and benefits is called critical thinking. By teaching him to use critical thinking, you will enable him to use the power of rational thought to help him through tough situations for the rest of his life.

Why Critical Thinking?

Your son will be faced with many decisions in his life. Some decisions are easy enough and do not require much thought.

Other decisions are life changing, and it is these that require critical thinking skills. Teaching your son how to gather information and analyze it carefully will help him cope in high-pressure situations.

 Fact

Teen boys are not well known for their ability to stop and reason about a decision. You need to deliberately set out to teach your son these skills. The earlier you start, the faster your son will learn to think through his options.

Critical thinking encompasses several vital steps:

- Observing an issue or determining a problem
- Asking questions and gathering facts about the issue
- Using the facts to draw conclusions and form options for dealing with an issue
- Using logic to assess the options and make arguments for or against each option
- Reaching a decision

These steps will help him in making any decision, big or small. Consider writing them down for your son or helping explain them in a way that makes sense to him.

Incorporating Critical Thinking

Once your son has the basics of the steps for critical thinking in his head, he has to put them into play. It is probably a good idea to spend some time role-playing with made-up situations and running through the steps with him. You can start by doing this together. Then you need to step back and let him tackle a couple of problems himself.

One of the best ways to teach these steps to your son is to talk to him about real-life situations as they come up. Invite him to help you work through a real problem using the critical thinking steps. As he comes up with issues in his life, remind him of the steps and let him know that you are always available to help him.

🄴 *Essential*

Emotions can really cloud anyone's mind, and your son needs to be aware of this. Remind him that when he is upset, excited, or feeling any other extreme emotion, he should take a time out to decide rationally what steps need to be taken.

Compassion

Compassion is the awareness of someone else's suffering and a desire to relieve that suffering. While the definition makes compassion seem like a passing thought, the truth is it is an action. This is a critical piece of your son's character.

Nurturing Compassion

Teenagers as a whole seem to be very unaware of others. Typically, teenagers aren't deliberately self-absorbed, but this self-focus is what helps them grow and prepare for leaving home. It becomes a parent's job to point out others and their suffering.

You might hear about a fire or a natural disaster on the news. Start a conversation with your son about how the people affected by the disaster might feel. What do they need to do to heal physically and emotionally? Ask him how he thinks others can help. This is one way to help him develop a sense of others. It might be easier for him to understand the needs of those close to him, such as people in your community.

The Act of Being Compassionate

For most parents it is more practical to define compassion as an act rather than an emotion. This means that you will have to find a way to encourage your son to undertake compassionate acts. The easiest way to do this is to find something that he is passionate about—a cause with his name on it.

 Alert

Do not panic if your compassionate teen takes on an issue that is very large or very far away from home. Many teens manage to do some truly incredible things, and one teen's idea could generate thousands of dollars for disaster relief half a world away. Help your son in any way you can.

If this fails, you can also encourage him to join you as you do compassionate acts. Remember this isn't just about giving money, though fundraising is one way to participate. It can be helping to rebuild a neighborhood hit by a natural disaster, recording books for the blind, or serving a meal at a homeless shelter. It doesn't really matter what your son does, as long as he does something.

Empathy

Empathy is the art of being able not only to be concerned with others, but also to attempt to put yourself in their shoes. This can be very hard for many young teens, but as your son gets older, it does become easier. Empathetic individuals often respond better when they recognize friends or relatives are in need of help.

Why Empathy Is Important

A study in *Adolescence* shows that empathy, intelligence, creativity, and reality testing are indications of emotional stability. Empathy is a skill your son has to learn. Empathy is a way to help your son in nearly every future interpersonal relationship. The ability to be able to see how another person might feel will help him plan his next move.

Empathy is a quality that cannot be taught, unlike riding a bike or dividing fractions, but parents can encourage empathetic behavior through their own words and actions. Ask your son small questions and move up to role-playing as he gains the maturity to handle empathy.

Look for opportunities to talk about empathy. Your son might mention something he saw at school or in the neighborhood, an altercation or dialogue between a student and teacher. Ask him to try to speak from both sides of the action. How did the participants feel? What might they have been thinking? How did their thoughts and feelings influence their behavior? How would he have handled it?

These types of questions will help your son learn to see how thoughts and feelings influence peoples' actions. This is something you should try to do often. Your son might enjoy these mind games, and they will provide him with human insight. It is also wise to teach your son not to overuse empathy. Remind him that it's possible project feelings that don't exist, and he needs to temper his beliefs of someone's feelings with reality.

Tolerance

As your son's world expands, he will encounter new people, ideas, and situations. It is important for him to be able to take in these experiences with an open mind. It is human nature to instinctively distrust the unfamiliar, but teaching your son the value of acceptance will help him become a well-rounded individual. The first step is to curb negative attitudes.

Prejudice at Home

Believe it or not, many prejudices start at home. You need to monitor carefully everything your son sees, does, or hears in your home. Here are some questions to ask yourself about prejudice in your home:

- Do you tell jokes of a religious or racial nature?
- Do you show movies that portray prejudice?
- Do you allow others to make remarks that slur others?

All of these can have detrimental effects on your son. By teaching him to respect everyone, you are doing what you can to help prevent him from being prejudiced, though this is only half the battle. You must also open the lines of dialogue. Be willing to have conversations about how others feel. Openly discuss biases people may have against your son because of his race, religion, or anything else. Talk to him about how he would feel about this and how you expect him to handle it.

E Essential

If you catch your son telling off-color jokes or displaying prejudice, address it immediately. Figure out why he said it and talk to him about what made it offensive.

Peer Groups

Teens tend to run in groups or crowds. Running with a specific set of people is one way your son defines himself. This group mentality is very important to your son. The problem is that once he identifies with his group, he may feel differently toward other groups.

It is important for you to teach your son that while his group of friends is great, he needs to remember that he shouldn't put other groups down. Just because other groups are different doesn't mean that they are bad or wrong. His group doesn't benefit from putting down another group; life simply doesn't work this way.

Volunteerism

Helping others is a great way for your son to learn about himself and lend a hand to those who may need help. Volunteering boosts self-esteem in many young people and is a chance to see things they may not be regularly exposed to.

Promoting Volunteerism

There is a never-ending supply of places that need help. You can help your son find the best place for him by looking at his strengths and passions.

 Fact

Your son should enjoy his volunteer work. If he doesn't, try to find out why. Help him find solutions to his issues, but also remind him of the length of his commitment and that he must follow through as long as he is not being harmed.

When considering locations to volunteer, consider the following issues:

- Location of the task
- Skills required for the task
- People involved with the task
- Hours required for completion of the task
- Length of commitment
- Training involved

- Safety of the location and task
- Any other requirements

Let your son have the final say after you have discussed the pros and cons of each volunteer opportunity. Talk with him about the benefits of certain forms of training and his desires and goals for the future. For example, if he wants to be a teacher, volunteering as a chess coach or reading teacher at a local elementary school may be a great fit. If your son wants to be a writer, he could volunteer to help at a senior center by organizing a community-based newspaper. If he wants to be a veterinarian, he can help at the local animal shelter.

Service Hours

Schools understand the value of helping others and what it teaches young men. In fact, many schools have organizational requirements for students to volunteer for a set number of hours each semester. Other schools have extracurricular organizations that are based on volunteer work.

E *Essential*

Many colleges want their applicants to have volunteer experience. While this is completely appropriate, you need to try to ensure that your son is doing his volunteering for the right reasons, not because he feels required to.

If the organization is service based, the number of hours may be great. Some schools have a thirty- to fifty-hour service requirement per semester. This is a lot of hours, but it can be met in many different ways. Have your son talk to the advisor to see if any activities he is currently volunteering in will count. Creativity and flexibility are important here.

Religion and Spirituality

The belief in something bigger than you is a powerful force for many adults. The feelings a teen has can be quite different. While many teens do think that they are nearly indestructible, many also enjoy a sense of spirituality and religion.

Organized Religion

Religion is an important part of many people's lives. No matter which religion you and your family are a part of, research shows that faith affects teens positively, through an increase in self-esteem or a drop in the use of drugs.

 Fact

In the teen years, your son may seem to pull away from organized religion or the religion that he has been raised with in your home. If he wants to explore other religions, offer to go with him or send him with friends.

The social and peer groups that are part of your religious or spiritual organization tend to echo your philosophy. Having your values reiterated in another location can be a very big boost for you. In any case, be sure your son knows that he can always talk to you if he hears something he doesn't agree with—your religion doesn't trump your son.

Negative Aspects of Religion

Some studies have found that religious involvement did not help teens when they felt that their religion chastised them or looked down on them. This rejection can lead to an increase in depression in teens.

Ⓔ *Essential*

Fighting about getting up in the morning to go to services is probably not high on anyone's list. If you are having trouble getting your son out of bed, consider trying a service at a different time. You get the benefits without the fight.

To ensure that your son is having a positive experience with organized religion, be sure to stop and talk to him. Does he go to services regularly? Is he a part of a youth group? Do you know who is in charge of activities for your son's age group? You should also make sure you know what your son is learning and doing when hanging out with the youth group.

More Religious than You

Your son may find he feels more religious than you do. Perhaps you don't attend any kind of services or only attend at major holidays. Your son may find friends who attend a local service and include him. You have to decide how you feel about that, especially if your son becomes involved in a religion you don't share.

It can be difficult for your son to attend services you know nothing about. You may not be interested in going with him regularly, but check them out to help him realize he has your blessing.

If the religion or service is something you aren't comfortable with, talk to your son about your feelings. Before you do so, ask yourself why you don't feel right about it. Don't jump to conclusions without trying it out and talking to your son. Religious differences can be painful for families, but working together with an open dialogue is what your son needs.

Spirituality

Your son's spirituality consists of his personal beliefs, his idea of the purpose of his life. He may or may not express this through religion, as religion is not necessary for an individual to feel spiritual. This sense of purpose may drive your son to be a good person and help him develop a good character.

Occasionally there are things that will rock your son's foundation. A crisis of faith or belief can be caused by any number of events, including the death of a family member or friend, an illness in himself or someone close to him, or sometimes even world events that seem out of control. Help him through the crisis by talking to him or helping him find someone else to talk to.

He may need space to work through his feelings on his own. As a parent, you may find it difficult to realize that you are not always able to protect him, but that is part of growing up. You can do your best to instill strong values in him and trust he will know how to apply them to his daily life.

Chapter 8

Developing a Sense of Responsibility

A sense of responsibility is very important for your son. He will rely on the foundations you lay now to help him learn to manage the tasks of everyday life as an adult. As he chooses his own activities, makes his own plans, and earns his own money, your son will have to learn not to rely on you to keep track of where he's supposed to be at what time.

Time Management for Teens

Time is a problem for most people. Learning how to manage your time as a teenager can make life a lot easier as an adult. It also gives teens a sense of ownership over their time.

Time Flies!

Time can get away from us easily. This is particularly true for teens. You used to keep your son's social and school calendar, ferrying him to play dates and reminding him of project due dates. He has to begin to accept that responsibility. Your son should start by making a list of all the things he must do, including school and home responsibilities. Then he is to make a separate list of things he wants to do. This might be playing a sport, hanging out with friends, or playing on the computer. Then he needs to add in time for sleep, eating, and hygiene. He should figure out how much time he needs to do each of these. This can be overwhelming. It might be helpful to use a pie chart and break it up into a twenty-four-slice pie to represent each of the twenty-four hours in a day.

E-Fact

As if you need another reason to tell your son to clean his room, working in an organized environment is a key way to maximize efficiency. He'll be able to work much more quickly if he knows exactly where to find everything he needs.

Writing down a schedule is a good way to help your teen get a handle on prioritizing. He will be able to see how his schedule will be affected if he makes last-minute plans or accepts additional responsibilities. Make sure he knows he cannot simply commandeer his sleep time to make room for more activities. It might sound like a good idea, but functioning on too little sleep means he will accomplish even less.

Scheduling for Teens

The truth is that many teens are overscheduled. Between school, social life, homework, and after-school activities, your son's life is full. As he learns to juggle all of these, he can also learn the importance of choosing what he will and won't do in the interests of time and sanity.

 *Essential*

Buy your son a teen-friendly calendar. Some calendars have spaces to write little details. If such a calendar feels overwhelming for him, buy him a very simple calendar. Also add a family calendar to your home, where people can easily check for conflicts.

The teen years are a great time to show your son respect by giving him some control over his schedule. But in doing so, he also needs to be respectful by checking his schedule with the family's schedule. One of the hard lessons to learn is that sometimes other people's business supersedes your own.

Building a Work Ethic

Work ethic is what helps motivate and drive your son. A work ethic is usually learned rather than innate. It is about his motivation to get a job done, be it a physical task, schoolwork, or something else he is interested in for pleasure.

Success and Failure

Your son will need a good role model to learn about success. Ideally, that would be you. You should show him that working hard to reach a goal is admirable. Your son also needs to know that as he works toward his goals, failure will happen. The key to making a failure into something positive is through the lessons learned. He will learn to gauge when to push himself harder to accomplish a goal.

If your son finds he likes the taste of success, he will try harder to obtain success in everything he does. He will carry this work ethic into his adult life. You cannot step in and save him. He needs to learn to deal with his own struggles, with you on the sidelines.

Waning Motivation

As your son becomes a teen, you may find that a previously good student is now not so interested in his studies. This is a fairly typical scenario.

 Alert

Colleges occasionally revoke acceptance letters at the end of high school. This happens when students succumb to senioritis and drop or fail courses. What your son does after being accepted to his college of choice is extremely important.

As your son grows, you lose the ability to control when or how he works on his school projects. It is time for your son to figure out how to get his tasks done on time and on his own terms. He will have to suffer from natural consequences if he does not do his work. He will learn, through his own work ethic, what it takes to complete tasks. This doesn't mean you shouldn't be supportive. He absolutely needs the tools to be successful, and it is your job to provide them—be they paper and pens or helpful advice and constructive criticism.

Once your son has found out what works for him, let him continue on his own. You will find that once he discovers what works for him or zeroes in on something that excites him, he will be much better off. He will motivate himself.

Earning and Respecting Privacy

Teens demand more privacy, and parents have a hard time estimating how much their child deserves. There has to be a happy medium between allowing your son room to grow and keeping an eye on him to ensure his health and safety.

How Much Privacy

Privacy allows your son to learn and grow. It gives him space to think and work through issues on his own. Having time and space to himself ensures that no one else is crowding him or just plain annoying him.

 Fact

You and your son have established a foundation of mutual trust and respect. You will lose all of this if you snoop. But you can suspend his right to privacy if you suspect your son is doing something very harmful and will not confess to it.

The issue becomes a problem when your son completely withdraws. While he may do this in the name of privacy, there is a difference between a healthy growing space and total isolation. As a parent, you are the best person to make the call on how much is too much alone time. Many professionals say that to gauge this, parents must look at their son's social networks and mannerisms when he is out of his room.

When He Loses Privacy

There are warning signs for parents to look for when trying to decide that their son has too much privacy. These signs may include:

- Bad grades
- Changes in weight
- Changes in friends
- Changes in social life
- Lifestyle changes, including sleeping and eating habits

 *Essential*

Granting privacy may be very hard for you if your son has broken your trust before, but it is important that you allow him to earn back this privilege. Set up the rules and start slowly.

While warning signs may call for some action, you may not need to take away all privacy. There still has to be some modicum of privacy, assuming there is no immediate risk of harm to your son. When you aren't sure what to do, it is always wise to seek the help of a mental health practitioner for advice.

Cash or Credit: Managing Money

Today's teens have more money than any other generation. This money can be a blessing or a curse. It all depends on how you as a parent teach your son to use his money. Abuse of money can be very dangerous, particularly for a teen, because it will follow him his whole life.

 Alert

Teens spent more than $53 billion dollars more in 2004 than they did in 1997. This amounts to about $175 billion, according to Teen Research Unlimited. Your teen needs to figure out how to spend his share wisely.

How to Manage Money

Teach money management early and often. By the time he is a teen, your son should have a good working knowledge of the meaning of most money management terms, such as credit, savings, interest, and the like.

Allowance is one method you can use to teach your son about money. While it is important for him to have money to allocate as he wishes, it is really the education behind the money that counts. Rather than simply handing over some money to your son at regular intervals, you need to teach him what to do once you let go of the cash.

About 30 percent of teens have a checking account. This teaches them to balance a checkbook, though your son also needs to understand the concept of a savings account. The majority of financial planners advise that a set portion of every single paycheck needs to go to savings, even when times are tough. This is one lesson that will stay with him his whole life.

Credit Basics

As many as 11 percent of thirteen- to fourteen-year-olds carry a credit card, according to a recent Junior Achievement poll. While this may help your son in an emergency situation or prevent him from losing his lunch money, there are other ramifications of credit cards for teens. You should define the term "emergency" for your son. An emergency is not when the team wins a game and everyone wants pizza.

 Fact

Credit is of growing importance. Many employers are now checking job applicants' credit ratings before they hire new employees. This makes protecting your credit even more important than ever.

If your teen has a credit card, he may not understand he is borrowing against future money. Make sure he knows about the credit card's grace period, late payments, and over-limit fees. He needs to understand that what he spends today will come back to him when the bill arrives in the mail. While many teens do pay their bills in full when their credit card statement comes, about 18 percent do not. This practice can set him up for a potentially overwhelming problem in the future. It is important to explain credit scores to your son.

Discuss interest rates, additional credit card fees, and credit limits, and teach your son to weigh the touted benefits with the potential money drains. Let him know how and where to check his credit report.

His First Job

Many teens will want to have a job. About half the teens who work do so in the retail industry. It is your responsibility to help your son find work appropriate for him.

Your son can reap many benefits by having a job. He will be able to earn some money, and he may learn new skills or meet new people, including the beginning of his employment network. A job will also provide him with the opportunity to learn responsibility.

Learning Responsibility

A job is a great way for teens to learn responsibility. Your teen will be responsible for getting to work, scheduling his work hours, and balancing work with school and his social life. Your job is to act as a lifeguard.

You should step in if there are problems. The problems might be workplace issues like an unsafe working environment or infractions of child labor laws as defined by your state.

You may also step in if you notice his grades and schoolwork are suffering.

You can make a case for having your son reduce the number of hours he works per week or even quit the job. After all, your son's most important job responsibility at this point in his life is getting a good education.

Earning Money

You may get really excited when your son announces that he wants a job. Perhaps you imagine your days of paying his bills are over. Maybe he is getting a job because you've told him he needs to pay for something specific, like his own car insurance. You have to realize that even with a great job, most teens do not earn a lot of money.

 Fact

> Your son needs to know practical information, like how to fill out a W-4 and what it means. You can find information on your teen's first job and tax tips at *www.hrblock.com/taxes/tax_tips/tax_planning/kids_firstjob.html.*

Having his own income will help your son learn to watch his money. This lesson is much easier to learn now than later when he is dependent on his paycheck for rent and groceries. A paycheck will also give you a chance to talk about taxes, social security, and perhaps union dues or fees for other associations.

Big Boys and Their Big Toys

When your son was younger, he was probably happy with small cars and trucks, perhaps a few blocks thrown in for good measure. However, as he grows, the size and price of his toys will probably increase as well.

Teen Toys

Your son probably has a wish list of items a mile long. You might not mind some of the items on that list, but others might be a shock to your wallet. Your son may want the items because of a sense of popularity or technology.

 Alert

> Despite what your son says, he is not going to die if he doesn't have the latest and greatest items. He may be angry or sad, but he will not be in mortal peril. Going without something he wants might teach him a lesson about saving money.

Affording Toys

Your son's list and your wallet probably don't match. That means you will have to say no to his wants. This is an important but difficult lesson for your son. You will have to explain to him about wanting versus needing.

You can also use this opportunity to open the conversation up about saving money to buy some of the items on his list. Show him how to make a plan to earn the money and save it to buy the item he wants most. This helps him feel ownership of the item and may make him less likely to lose it or break it through carelessness.

 *Alert*

Technology makes it possible for teens who want things to steal them without leaving home. Illegally pirated music, videos, and video games proliferate on the Internet. Your son must know this is wrong and you won't stand for it.

Home Alone as a Latchkey Kid

Leaving your son alone at home is a big step and not one for which every parent or every teen feels ready. Only you and your son can decide what works best for your family.

Is Your Son Ready?

Experts in childcare usually agree it is best to never leave your child alone until the age of twelve. However, find out if your state or city has laws that determine how old your child must be before you leave him without adult supervision.

Here are some questions to answer to help you decide if your son is ready to be at home alone:

- Is your son responsible?
- Is everything okay between you and your son?
- Does your son know where to go and who to call in an emergency?

- Do you trust your son?
- Is your son willing to stay home alone?

There may be times when your son is fine being home alone, but you may have to reevaluate your decision periodically. There may be times when he is not able to stay alone because of behavioral or emotional issues. Be sure that you have a backup plan, should a change be necessary.

Setting the Rules for Alone Time at Home

A big question when deciding whether to leave your son home alone is how he will behave when you aren't there. One of the best ways to make sure your son won't do anything you disapprove of is to give him explicit written rules to follow. This ensures that there won't be any miscommunications.

E *Essential*

You should always have any weapons in the home locked up. Always store ammunition in a separate place. Your son should not have access to the weapons, ever. This is a tragedy waiting to happen.

Address issue of how he is to spend his time. Be clear and specific about the rules of not only what he needs to do, but also what he should not be doing.

Another hot topic for teens is who can be in the house when you aren't home. Many parents have rules that say no friends or girlfriends allowed when the parents aren't home.

The stakes go up if your son is also expected to take care of younger siblings. Some activities, like cooking and bathing younger children, increase the risks of accidents, so be cautious about asking your teen to do them alone.

The American Red Cross offers a teen babysitting course. This will teach your son the best way to handle infants and young children as well as give him some safety advice. This emergency preparation will come in handy for everyone's peace of mind.

Chapter 9

Social Issues

Teens are social creatures by nature. This means a dizzying array of friends and other acquaintances. Your son's social connections will help him define who he is and learn to deal with life. The relationships he forms as a teen will be more adult in nature than those he had as a young child, and his teachers will demand he be more accountable for his work. All of these factors contribute to your son's social skills.

Being an Individual

One of the first lessons your son will need to learn is how to separate himself from others. He learned when he was younger to separate himself from you. Now it is time for him to figure out how to become an individual.

An Individual among the Masses

You may have noticed that most teens are very similar in how they dress and behave—but that doesn't mean they are all clones with no capacity for individual thought.

It is important that your son knows he is a unique individual, despite his clothing or outward behavior. He has his own voice, and you can help him figure out how to express his opinions. He should be encouraged to experiment with whatever his heart desires, as long as it is safe. Feeling this sense of freedom to be different can also lead him to respect himself and help him find his creativity and skills that are uniquely his.

Ⓔ *Question*

What if my son wants to be very different?
It is important to encourage individuality. He may have political or social reasons or he may just be defiant. It's healthy for your son to express his individuality, but you may need to step in if it interferes with his school work or relationships.

Unique—but Not Too Unique

As important as it is to be unique, it is equally important for most teens to not stick out like a sore thumb. This means that as a teen your son will have a certain amount of pack mentality. This will decrease as he gets older and becomes more comfortable being himself.

You can expect to hear exactly what other kids are wearing and doing. It is a kid version of keeping up with the Joneses. Encourage your son to find a way to walk that line of being in the group and yet distinct. This might mean taking baby steps—wearing the same brand of shoe but in a different color.

Manners for Young Men

There is nothing as nice as seeing a young man with manners. The question is how to make sure your teen is one of them!

Teaching Manners

Manners mean a lot of different things to different people. For some it is purely about how you behave at the table. Other people define manners as how you interact with others on a daily basis, including the physical etiquette of meeting people, dining, dancing, and the like. How your family defines manners is a personal decision and will be based on your traditions and values.

 *Essential*

If you are looking for a fun way to teach your son some manners, there are always etiquette classes. Check your local Yellow Pages for etiquette schools in your area.

By showing your son the behavior you expect, it will become second nature to him. Good manners will also help him appear mature to other adults. This can be a big plus, particularly in the middle of a group of other teen boys.

Where Did the Manners Go?

Let's face it, when you're a teenage boy, there will be slip-ups when it comes to manners. This might include loud and rowdy behavior. Many teens also use vulgar language. You need to decide what is acceptable and what is out of bounds.

Once you decide what the infractions are, you will also have to decide the punishments. There may be different punishments for varying degrees of rudeness. It is completely different to belch at the table than to be rude to a teacher. You should let your son know you expect him to follow the rules of manners both in your home and outside of it.

Awareness of Others

Teenagers are often known for being self-centered. As your son grows, he will learn to realize that there are other people who matter when it comes to making decisions. He'll also need to learn to consider others before he opens his mouth.

Observing and Learning

Developing a sense of what someone else is thinking or feeling is important. It can help your son learn to gauge his reactions and think ahead.

Ⓔ *Essential*

Try to involve your son in some family decisions. This can be something small, like where to go for dinner, or it can be a larger issue, like planning a family vacation. This lets him know his opinion matters.

The first step is for your son to realize that there are other people who matter. If your son can accurately determine how someone is feeling, he can respond appropriately. If someone is angry, he can examine what is going on and make a decision to help that person work through his or her anger or remove himself from the situation. This can help protect his own feelings as well.

How to Develop Awareness

One of the easiest ways to show your son that others are important is to talk about how consideration for others works in your life. You might start by explaining to him a decision you are currently mulling over. Let's say you are trying to plan your vacation. You explain that you need to find a good time to visit your vacation spot, and you also need to ensure your job is covered so your co-workers aren't left high and dry.

Your son should try to put this into practice. He will inevitably have to work in a group for a school project, and this is a good time to point out how his actions or failures to act play a part in the other group members' lives. This can be a very hard lesson for teens to learn. Teens tend to be very self-promoting and unaware of others.

Dealing with Anger

Anger is the emotional response to frustration. Teens can respond to anger by physically lashing out or by bottling up their rage. Neither way is healthy, and parents need to teach their children how to work through their anger constructively.

Dealing with Anger

Since you have known your child his whole life, you can easily pick up on his warning signs. Your son's powers of perception may not be so keen, and he may be unable to immediately identify anger when he feels it. Having the ability to recognize anger in himself is a very important skill. When he loses his temper, let him cool off and then talk to him. Ask him if he realized what he was doing when he lashed out. Doing this can help him recognize his own anger in the future, which is the first step to coping with it.

 Fact

Teen anger may come out as rage or sarcasm, indifference or quietness. Anger does not cause destruction unless it is dealt with improperly—such as when it is allowed to escalate into hostility or aggression, when it is ongoing, or when it's kept in and not addressed.

Teens deal with anger in different ways. There isn't one right way to respond, but your son needs to realize that there are multiple ways to deal with his anger. Suggest that he:

- Cool off by physically removing himself from the situation
- Stop and try to communicate, which includes listening to the other person
- Realize that his thought process may be compromised by anger
- Use relaxation skills, like counting to ten

- Exercise if he feels anger or frustration building up; the release of endorphins can make him feel better
- Listen to music to help him relax and sort through his feelings

When Anger Is a Problem

Anger can be a problem when it seems pervasive in your son's life or when it is mismanaged. If teaching him the skills to deal with his anger doesn't work, it may be time for professional help. You may also need professional help if your son is in danger of harming himself or others, if his anger leads to depression, or if he is destroying property, hurting animals, or engaging in other worrisome behaviors.

Bottled-up anger is a real problem. Suppressed anger can lead to other problems for your son, including depression, hostility, and cynicism. If you see that your son is constantly being critical, or is passive-aggressive or depressed in general, it is time to talk to your health care provider. There are classes available for anger management that are designed to help teens overcome anger issues and move forward.

How to Be a Good Friend

Teenage friendships are very important. They can provide great learning experiences as well as painful missteps. Your son may have outgrown his earlier friendships or you may see the same faces scarfing down snacks in your kitchen. Regardless of how long your son has known his friends, the nature of his friendships will become more adult in his teenage years.

What Is a Friend?

Defining the characteristics of a good friend is one of the most challenging aspects of adolescence. Your job is to help him identify the attributes he values in his friends.

You can lead by example, but it may also be appropriate to have a conversation with your son about the qualities of a good friend. Having him make a list and helping him add and subtract items may be one way to have him see the qualities of a good friend. Once he knows what he is looking for in a friend, he has something to emulate.

Anti-Social Teens

It can be very difficult to see your son seemingly friendless. First, ask yourself why you believe he doesn't have friends. Is it because he doesn't bring people over, gab on the phone, or go out? While these may be indicators, it's also possible that he isn't bringing his friends around for you to meet.

 Fact

It is very important that you know your son's friends. When possible, you should also try to reach out to the parents of his friends. He may see this as being overbearing or protective, but it's just a part of good parenting.

You might find out that your son has plenty of friends if you e-mail his favorite teacher or talk to the leader of his after-school club. This means he's avoiding having you interact with his friends. Try to find out why this is happening. It could be that he's embarrassed by you or it could simply be a timing issue; either way it's something you should be aware of to try to brainstorm a solution.

If your son truly does not have friends, you may want to figure out why. Is your son depressed? You might seek the advice of a school counselor or teacher who may see him in a more social setting. They can also help you determine if he needs professional help. Sometimes the solution is helping him find friends who share his interests. Suggest he get involved in after-school activities or clubs. Brainstorm ideas with your son to put him in a position to make friends.

Driving: The Rules and the Rights

Driving is serious business. It is definitely a responsibility and not a right. Your son needs to understand the important nature of driving and the responsibility that necessarily goes along with it.

Driving Dangers

Automobile-related deaths are the number one cause of death for teens. More than 40 percent of teen deaths in 2002 were related to driving, according to the research center ChildTrends. The good news is that lawmakers and parents are taking driving more seriously, even if teens aren't.

The number of teens who get their license at sixteen dropped by 25 percent between 1993 and 2003 due to new state licensing requirements. Most states now have graduated licensing requirements. This means there are longer learning periods, curfews, and restrictions on behavior, including how many people can be in the car with your son during certain licensing periods.

Fact

Only about 60 percent of teens will get their driver's license at age sixteen. Only at age nineteen does the number reach 80 percent. This may contradict your beliefs or your son's statements about who is driving and who isn't.

Rules of the Road

Just as you have rules about everything else, you should have rules about the car. Getting a driver's license is not a right; do not allow your son to get his license if you don't feel he is ready for the responsibility. Your son should:

- Show responsibility in most situations
- Verbalize his understanding of road responsibilities
- Be trustworthy when alone in a car
- Understand what to do in an emergency situation
- Understand that alcohol and drugs are never allowed near the car—ever!

Once he has his license, you need to set rules for your son. A written contract is a great idea because it clearly lists everyone's responsibilities and the consequences if the rules aren't followed. Then there are no surprises for anyone. You also need to be sure to enforce the rules; driving is one place where there should be no second chances.

Rules might include:

- Who can ride with him
- Where he can drive
- When he can drive
- Which activities are allowed and which are prohibited while he is driving (such as playing the radio, talking on the phone, eating food, and so forth)

 Alert

Tell your son he can call on you no matter what the hour or what the problem. Remind him that his safety is your main concern. He should never ride in a car with someone who is intoxicated or drive if he is intoxicated.

Growing Autonomy

The ability to do things by oneself precedes independence. Once your son is able to do things on his own, he will have an easier time making decisions for himself. This is one of the hardest tasks of growing up. It can also be a difficult issue for parents; it is hard to let your child fly on his own because sometimes you have to watch him stumble.

Why Autonomy Is Important

Your son wants to make choices for himself. This starts very early in life. When he was a toddler, he may have snatched his clothes out of your hands and defiantly exclaimed, "No!

I'll do it!" Teenagers do the same thing. The difference is that the choices your son makes now have larger ramifications than wearing his shoes on the wrong feet. Basically, your son needs to learn to take care of himself. While he may have some of the basics down, like hygiene, it is important that he learn other tasks within the safety of your home.

How to Help Your Son

Your son will need to learn many tasks before leaving home. You should be sure to include:

- Budgeting
- Laundry
- Grocery shopping
- Basics of cooking
- House keeping (vacuuming, dusting, etc.)
- Writing a professional letter
- Conducting a professional telephone call

Your son may see your lessons on the mundane chores of adult life as a punishment. He has every right to think that, and to him it may feel like a truth. After all, you have done his laundry for all these years, and now you're asking him to do his own. Remind him it is not a punishment but rather a life skill.

Virtual Society: Texting, Chatting, E-mailing, and Blogging

The world is a much different place than when you were a child. Parents used to know everyone who lived on the street and knew if there was something to worry about. Now the boundaries teens face encompass not one street but the entire virtual and technological world. Your son may use his cell phone to chat and text message people; he may do homework and blog online—in short, there is no end to the possibilities for teens and technology these days.

Fact

An online survey by Teenage Research Unlimited showed nearly a quarter of teens in relationships have communicated with their boyfriend/girlfriend between midnight and 5 A.M. using a cell phone.

Teens find that there are an infinite number of things to do online. They may use it for scholastic purposes: homework, research, and reading school blogs. Many teachers use the Internet to post assignments and links. But your teen may also be blogging, chatting, and looking at objectionable material— or even posting objectionable material, including inappropriate pictures of himself or others. Be sure you have a plan in place for how to deal with these issues.

Parent as Octopus

Your teen has access to such a vast array of technology that it may seem overwhelming to you. This is something to keep in mind as you incorporate technologies into his life and yours. For example, while you may view a cell phone as a necessary tool for keeping tabs on your son, he can use his cell phone to call people, text message, and chat online—actions that are out of your control. These devices can be used for nefarious purposes—like finding drugs or arranging a way to sneak out of the house—and are harder than you think to track. Be wise and supervise any technology your son uses.

 Alert

If your son uses the Internet, chances are he has been to sites like *MySpace.com* or *Facebook.com*. These popular online communities connect your son to people he knows and some he doesn't. Establish rules for the proper use of these sites.

Staying Safe Online

One of the most important rules about keeping your son safe online is to know what he is doing. This may mean you need to take a class to become a bit more computer literate. This will help you know what your son does and what he talks about when it comes to being online.

 **Essential**

Teens like to find answers for themselves. The guide at the Teen Advice Web site (*www.teenadvice.about.com*) runs a clean site that is up-to-date and clear on many topics, yet written just for teens and their parents.

You should have firm rules about using the Internet and the other technologies associated with it. These rules should include what is acceptable and what is not as well as the consequences if the rules are broken. Some rules might include the following:

- No computers are allowed in teen bedrooms, only in common areas.
- Internet software is installed to track and/or block certain sites or keywords.
- The Internet is not used without a parent in the room.
- Your son should never post any personal information online.
- Your son will not link to pages of others who give this information away.
- Your son will only use certain approved sites and technologies.
- There are time limits and hours of operation.
- Your son may not physically meet with anyone he met online.
- Your son should tell a parent immediately if anyone online makes him feel uncomfortable.

Make sure your son knows that these rules are for his own safety, not to make his life unnecessarily complicated. He must understand that using the Internet is a privilege; it's a fun and useful tool, but it can also be abused.

Chapter 10

School Issues

Your son needs a good education to make it in life. This education can come in many ways, though the most common is traditional schooling. Your role has changed since your son first started school. Your relationship with his teachers is probably much more distant, and your son has to keep track of his own assignments and due dates.

Homework Hassles

Homework is an important part of school, yet it can be the bane of a parent's existence. You may feel like you spend a lot of time helping your son with homework or arguing over it.

How to Do Homework

Your son needs to have an area set up specifically for homework, either in his room or in a common area. Stock it with supplies he will need and books he might find useful, like a dictionary or thesaurus. Keeping his homework supplies handy will prevent him from coming up with excuses to stop doing work. If your homework center is in a common area, it may include a computer. Your son will spend a lot of time in his area, so he should have some say in the comforts. The chair and desk you bought when he entered first grade may not be best now, and his comfort level will affect his productivity.

While your son should work steadily, he should also take breaks every twenty minutes. Watching an hour-long television show is not a break. Tell your son to stand and stretch or walk around; this will help him stay alert for longer assignments. Teach him to find the natural breaks, but a timer is a great way to remind him if he tends to work straight through.

 Fact

The U.S. Department of Education says middle school kids spend about two hours on homework each evening and teens in high school can handle more than two hours per day. If you think your child has too much homework, check with the teacher to see how long the work is expected to take.

Let your son know that you are available to help him, but leave him alone while he does his homework. When he asks for help, do not give him the answers right away. Give him the tools or resources he needs to answer his question by himself. Guide him, and let him figure things out for himself.

Don't Fight over Homework

As tempting as it is, do not fight over your son's grades. You need to give your son the tools he needs to do well and go from there. One of the easiest things to do is to help him determine the best schedule for him to do his homework. Sit down and pick out which hours will be devoted to homework each night. Since he will help you and state his preferences, he will be committed to following the rules.

Essential

> Homework is your son's responsibility. He needs to do it himself. You should not stand over him and tell him what to do or how to do it. Occasional advice is just that—occasional. Be sure to let your son have ownership of his work.

By giving your son input, you will allow him to help design something that will reflect his learning styles. Homework schedules can be adjusted for times before tests and the like. Your son may enjoy studying with friends as well. This can be a brilliant idea for some kids. Consider hosting them at your house. Many parents say their sons want to listen to music or the television while studying. This may prove to be a help and not a hindrance. If he's putting forth the effort, it must be working. It can also make his hours of studying more pleasant.

Finding Learning Styles and Differences

Learning differences can be something as simple as trying to figure out what type of learning method works best for your son. If he has a learning disorder, you will have to take special care to tailor his study methods to deal with it; the first step is having the disorder properly diagnosed. Many learning differences aren't discovered until middle school. Since you know your son the best, you might be the first to realize that he learns differently from his siblings or peers.

Pinpointing Differences

Everyone has a way that he or she learns best. Most people fall into one of three categories:

- **Visual Learner:** Learns by seeing. Videos, posters, books, and physical demonstrations are useful tools.
- **Auditory Learner:** Learns by hearing material or information. Lectures and listening to a recording are primary tools.
- **Tactile Learner:** Learns by physically experiencing the material. Role-playing, touching, and experimenting are sound methods.

Each of these learning styles processes material in a distinct way. It can be hard for teachers to gear lessons toward all three types of learners. If you know your son is one type of learner, a quick call or e-mail to his teacher can help both of you to brainstorm the best way for him to learn. This also shows the teacher that you are paying attention and are interested. If addressing learning styles doesn't seem to help, then there may be more going on than a simple teacher/pupil mismatch. There are some signs to watch for in your son, such as:

- A slow pace when working
- Inattention to details

- Poor organizational skills
- Inability to understand what he has just read
- Poor memorization skills
- Inability to understand the abstract
- Inability to adapt to change
- Difficulty with understanding directions
- Making careless mistakes
- Avoidance or dislike of schoolwork

Thriving with a Learning Disability

According to the U.S. Department of Education, about 5 percent of all students enrolled in public schools have a learning disability. A learning disability is not the result of poor parenting or other environmental concerns. It is also not the same as mental retardation. There are many types of learning disabilities, including dysgraphia (writing disorder), dyslexia (reading disorder), dyscalculia (mathematical disorder), dyspraxia (motor coordination disorder), and apraxia (motor speech disorder). Attention deficit disorder (ADD) can also affect your son's learning. This may also come with the symptom of hyperactivity, known as attention-deficit hyperactivity disorder or ADHD.

Essential

The National Center for Learning Disabilities (NCLD) is a great resource for all ages. Its Web site (*www.ncld.org*) not only provides information on the diagnosis but on testing and treatment for all ages and all learning disabilities.

If you think your son has a learning disability, seek professional testing from your health care practitioner. This may include conversations and assessments by you, his teachers, and health care professionals. Diagnosing a learning disability is the first step to treating it. This may include therapy, life adaptations, or potentially medications. Sometimes a combination of all these methods is what your son needs.

How to Talk to Teachers

Talking to teachers and other school officials is an important task of parenting. Sometimes it can be difficult to get over the feeling of uneasiness that comes with sitting in the principal's office, even as the parent.

Parental Involvement

Studies show that students whose parents are involved tend to earn higher grades. This does not necessarily mean baking cookies and attending PTA meetings, though.

Many parents wait until issues arise to get involved. If you operate this way, you won't have an established relationship with your son's teachers when you need it. If you meet your son's teachers at conferences or from being involved at school, it will be easier to deal with problems if they come up. It also shows the teacher that you really care, and teachers may come to you earlier in the process.

What to Say to a Teacher

While it is imperative that your son learn to handle the daily discussions with his teachers, there is a time and a place for parental involvement. Sometimes your advice and guidance are all your son needs to talk to a teacher. This is a great time to try role-playing as a way to help your son.

Ⓔ *Question*

Can I send notes to my son's teacher?
E-mail works perfectly for this type of communication, and you don't have to rely on your son as the delivery person. Tell the teacher who you are and that you want to help in any situation, good or bad. Ask how the teacher prefers to communicate and then do your best to stick with that method.

Your son may encounter a situation that requires parental involvement. This might be because the teacher is not listening to your son or because your son is unable to convey his concerns to the teacher. Call or e-mail the teacher to find a time that is mutually agreeable for you and the teacher to meet. Remember you only know your son's half of the story. Be inquisitive and not combative. Show the teacher that you want to find a solution. Bring your son in whenever possible.

Dealing with an Underachiever

If your son has trouble living up to your expectations or his own, you have an underachiever on your hands.

The Nature of Underachievers

Before you can begin to address the issue of what to do about your son's underachievement, you must figure out why he is underachieving. Is he unchallenged in school? Perhaps he has an emotional issue or something else that keeps him preoccupied, preventing anything else from breaking into his thoughts. Maybe he has an undiagnosed learning disability. All of these are potential reasons that your son might be an underachiever.

E Fact

Underachieving may carry over into sports or other activities in which your son once showed interest or aptitude. A complete drop in everything your son was interested in can be a sign of depression or substance abuse and warrants a referral to a mental health professional.

You may need help determining the reason for your son's lack of achievement. Start with your son. Ask him what is going on in his life. He may have an idea about what is wrong, or he may feel completely useless. Is there a pattern in his problem? For example, is it only one class? Ask teachers, coaches, or other leaders who may know your son if they can shed any light on his low achievement.

Making Changes

When you figure out what is going on with your son, you can try to make a difference to help him change. Help your son become willing to do the required work. To do this, you have to help him find the motivation inside himself.

The motivation to succeed can come from many places. It can be from the desire to get into a prestigious college or to attend a certain sports event and emerge victorious. The path of this desire is unimportant, but the lesson that he must be willing to work for his dreams is one that will last his whole life. This may be an uphill battle for both of you because old habits are hard to break. Be sure you give your son the emotional, mental, and physical support he needs.

Dealing with an Overachiever

While it sounds like a wonderful predicament to find yourself in, being the parent of an overachiever presents unique challenges.

Overachieving Versus Hardworking

Overachievers may be driven to perfection. How do you know if your son is an overachiever versus someone who works very hard?

One of the best ways to figure out if your son is merely working hard is to see how he responds to failures. Is his reaction proportionate to the problem? Does he think he can make changes in the future and do better next time or does he believe that his chances at an Ivy League school just went out the window with his latest AP calculus exam?

If your son has trouble figuring out where to be truly upset and where to buckle down and work harder, you may have a problem. You should try to see how pervasive this problem is. Is he this way only in school or does it also affect his life in sports, music, or other activities? The more areas of his life that are affected by this perfectionism, the bigger your problem.

 Fact

According to a UCLA Higher Education Research Institute study of 400,000 college freshman, about two-thirds reported spending an hour or less a night on homework. Children may not be as overworked as they think.

Teaching Your Son to Rein It In

While it may appear that a kid who is doing well has everything to live for, the research paints a very different picture of overachievers, who displayed increased rates of:

- Depression
- Eating disorders
- Suicidal thoughts and actions

Teach your son how to deal with his ideas and perceptions and how to handle them in a way that is not self-destructive. He needs to know that failures can breed success; mistakes are expected and present learning opportunities.

Dealing with Problems at School

School can be a huge source of problems. Teens may have trouble with academics or with their teachers or peers. The problems can begin to compound if they aren't addressed.

Problems with Scholastic Activities

The extent of the problems varies based on your son and the school. If you spot problems, it is always easier to deal with them right away rather than wait for them to explode.

Let your son try to resolve his school problems on his own. You are his secret weapon, only called out in the final stages when nothing else is working. Even if you are called in, remember that if your son is in the wrong, he is wrong. You both need to realize you cannot save him.

E Essential

Some teens are so excited by all the possibilities at high school that they try to do it all. This can be the downfall of many a well-meaning teen. Help your son find a happy medium.

Problems with Peers

Your son's social network or lack of it may cause problems for him in school. If your son is having problems with others, stay out of the fights. This does not mean you can't be involved in helping your son actively solve the problems, but do so from the sidelines. Also be leery of ever taking sides or disparaging his friends; when or if they make up, your words will hang in his ears for a long time.

You can help your son with a lack of peer relations by being available. Some parents enforce a rule that their son will be involved in at least one after-school activity. This exposes your son to other people his age. It also allows you to know something about who he is hanging out with during these hours.

You can influence these activities by making suggestions, but allow your son to have the final say. Once he does begin to attend, ask questions about the other kids. Be open to him inviting people into your home. This allows you to see the interaction and meet the other kids.

Having positive friendships outside of school can help your son realize that not everyone is like his peers at school. For kids who are very school-oriented, outside friendships can provide a new perspective and the opportunity to get to know different people.

Chapter 11

Outside Influences

You want your son to have great role models. You have ide-als that you want to impart to him. The truth is that while you do have a large amount of influence on your son, you're not alone. The competition for your son's attention is great, and you need to be sure to find the best place for him by guid-ing him to making the right decisions.

Who Has Power and Why?

Peer pressure is something many parents worry about. While you know that ultimately you can teach your son only so much before it's time for him to fly on his own, this is scant comfort when your worry reflex kicks in. Having a good base for your son is the most important thing you can give him.

Parents Are Key

You have influence over your son. This may come as quite a shock to you, but studies show that teens who have a good relationship with their parents are less likely to be in trouble and less likely to abuse drugs and alcohol. The relationship between parent and son is an important one, and it requires work. The time you spend in building a good relationship will help you nurture him until he is able to make decisions for himself. It also gives him the faith that you will be there to help him solve problems and issues that may arise.

Studies show that parents have more influence over their sons than peers do. This should ease your mind as a parent, though you shouldn't let your guard down. The rest of your family, especially your son's siblings, also influence the way he acts.

E Fact

If your son isn't testing the limits, you may have a bigger problem on your hands, like depression. If your son is testing limits, state the rules and the punishment for breaking them. Enforcement and consistency are the keys to successful boundaries.

Friends Contend

Research by Dr. Lianne Woodward in the *Journal of Abnormal Child Psychology* showed that preteens who had poor peer relations in the middle school age group were more likely to have problems as teenagers.

Friends are more important than the outer peer groups or his school in general. His close friends will have more influence than others. This means it is important to be sure that his friends have values and judgment that you would like to see in your son.

Friends

Friends are an important part of life. Your son will learn to relate to others outside of his family through his relationships with close friends.

Choosing Good Friends

You should teach your son to choose his friends wisely from an early age. You can accomplish this by talking to him about the characteristics you value in your friends. Your son will also observe your friends and your relationships with them for himself. As he gets older, talk to him about what he values in his friends. Let him articulate the qualities he looks for in his friends.

 *Essential*

Your son needs to learn how to cultivate friendships. This can take some practice, and you can encourage him to talk through his frustrations and work matters out.

Once your son has a list of qualities that he wants in his friends, ask him about his current friends. Do they have these qualities? What qualities does he like about his current friends? Friendships will help teach him conflict resolution and loyalty only if his friends have these qualities. If your son can't list the qualities, help him out.

If you think your son's friends do not embody the characteristics you would like to find in a friend, try to help him reach a conclusion himself. You might ask your son what he sees in a certain friend. If he says loyalty, ask him to define loyalty and whether the friend's actions line up with that definition.

What If You Don't Like His Friends

If you find that your son has gotten mixed up in a crowd or with a friend that doesn't have the qualities you deem acceptable, talk to your son first. Ask him to remind you about what he looks for in a friend. He may actually see these qualities in the friends that you don't like.

(E) Essential

Getting to know the other parents can be a very helpful tool. Denise Witmer of *www.parentingteens.about.com* advises that you call the other teen's parents. To break the ice, try to find something positive to say about their child.

It is usually easier to try to have your son around people you think are better friends for him. There are some guidelines to helping your son establish good friendships:

- Control situations with kids you're not sure of. Invite them over instead of letting your son go out.
- Be careful about making disparaging remarks about his friends; he may become defensive and less likely to see your point.

- Distinguish between activities and people when dealing with your dislikes as a parent.
- Give him more time, freedom, and money to be around kids you approve of.
- If your son's friends are endangering his life in any immediate way or are engaging in illegal behaviors, you should do your best to ensure they stay separate.

Inhibiting your son from hanging with his friends can create a rift in your relationship. Overlook those friends who are nothing more than nuisances. He'll grow out of them. However, if participation in a negative peer group leads him toward drug abuse, early sexual activity, violence, or other unwanted behaviors, it's time to intervene. Help him find another group. It's easier for him to give up the negative group if there is another group to join. Being part of a group is critical during the teen years—your son will not want to be the odd man out.

Peer Pressure

Peer pressure is a fact of life. Anytime we are around others, there is peer pressure. Sometimes this pressure is unspoken. Even if no one says anything to him, your son may feel pressure to act or dress a certain way simply because he watches how his peers act or dress. Peer pressure can also be expressed in words, and it's this form of pressure that parents think of when they hear the phrase.

What Does Peer Pressure Look Like?

Peer pressure takes many different forms. It can be a positive influence that says, "Hey, I know you're a smart guy—why aren't you getting good grades like we are?" Or it can be the negative version of, "If you weren't such a baby you'd smoke like the rest of us. Are you afraid?"

There are tricks that teenagers use to influence each other, and they can take the form of praise, putdowns, and verbal assaults.

The Benefit of Peers

Peer pressure is not always a bad thing. It can help your son learn the social norms for a particular group. Think about the first meeting of a sports or academic team. Your son hangs back long enough to figure out where everyone else is going and mimics their behavior. This is unspoken but teaches your son the expected behaviors.

 Fact

Get your son involved in charity work. This can help teach him the value of giving, and he can learn firsthand how good it feels to be a part of something positive.

Your son may also find that he is in a group that exerts peer pressure in a positive way. It may be that his group of friends all get good grades. Your son can be influenced by this in order to stay in the good graces of the group.

Handling Peer Pressure

The point of peer pressure is to get someone to change his behavior. This can be positive or negative. People cave in to peer pressure for a variety of reasons that include:

- Worries about social status
- Inability to make a decision
- Fear
- Desire to avoid hurt feelings
- Desire to appear mature

To learn to avoid peer pressure that makes him feel uncomfortable, your son needs some practice. Role-playing and pointing out various situations can work really well. Your son may have trouble believing that anyone he knows would try to encourage him to do something that wasn't right.

Ⓔ *Essential*

It is imperative that you teach your son to have a plan to recognize and deal with peer pressure. This will help him when the situation arises so that it need not be a crisis for him.

Your son needs to learn to be assertive in turning someone down. He shouldn't bother being aggressive or loud; this will only incite the other party. Teach him that a confident, firm stance will help him immensely. Should he find that a certain group is constantly pressuring him to do things he doesn't want to do, he will need to decide if it is worth the effort to maintain the friendships.

School

For most teenagers, going to school is something they have to do, rather than something they want to do. This doesn't mean your son doesn't have days or parts of school that he likes. But in general, it's something he'd probably rather skip. Even though this is true, it doesn't mean that school doesn't have some influence on your son.

 Fact

Boarding or military school is not always the answer for teens with problems. There are counselors and small programs like outdoor adventure programs designed for struggling teens. Be sure you have the approval of your son's mental health care provider before sending your son away.

What Does School Teach?

What your son's school teaches goes way beyond what is actually said or done in the classroom. At school, your son will pick up on cues about how learning is regarded, how other students are treated, and how he himself is treated.

School is a place where your son will come into contact with teachers and students. He will be exposed to opinions that differ from his own, and he will have to learn to cope with these differences. Make sure your school's vision for your son matches your own. If you want your son to go to college, make sure the teachers promote higher education. If you want your son to see his school as a resource for exploring the world, make sure the school is equipped to show it to him through extracurricular activities or out-of-classroom experiences. Ideally, your son's school will be a good academic fit for him as well as a place where his love of learning will be nurtured.

Finding the Right School

Some parents have the ideal school picked out before their child is even born. Sometimes the school is available and their son thrives in it, though it is not always that easy. Your son may dislike the school you have selected for academic or personal reasons. If it was your dream that he go to that particular school, it may be very hard for you to let go, but it is more important that your son be in the school that's right for him so that he can succeed.

Signs that your son is not enjoying school or is misplaced include your son's:

- Reluctance to go to school
- Poor grades
- Lack of friends
- Lack of participation in extracurricular activities, especially if the school offers activities that would normally appeal to him
- Faking illnesses to avoid school
- Talking about other schools
- Outright saying he dislikes this school

If your son is having a hard time at a school, your first point of action is to find out why. Perhaps there is something that can be solved without changing schools. If this is the case, make the changes and reevaluate the situation. If it doesn't help, evaluate viable alternatives for your son. He may have some insight, as might your local board of education.

 *Essential*

Teens fare better taking driving lessons at school or from a student driver program than they do with Mom or Dad riding shotgun. Look into your school's driver's education program.

Television and Movies

Television has become a way of life for many American families. The average American child will watch twenty-eight hours of television a week, more time than any other single activity with the exception of sleep. Whether your son watches movies or regular television programming, he sees an enormous amount of fictional life, and it may influence the way he feels he should look or behave.

Negativity and the Media

Aside from the sheer time your son will spend in front of a screen, there is real harm in watching violence in the media. Media violence has been linked to aggressive and violent behavior in teens. It also desensitizes children to violence and can make them feel insecure about the world in which they live.

 Fact

According to the American Academy of Pediatrics, your child will watch about 40,000 television commercials per year. Advertisers spend about $300 billion annually to influence how your teenager spends his money.

Aside from violent and anti-social behavior, television features gratuitous sex and materialism. Television standards have relaxed, and your son can view sex acts on regular primetime television, not to mention cable. By allowing your son access to these images, you can unintentionally contradict the messages you send to your son about your family values.

Is There Anything Good on Television?

Television and movies are not all horrible. They are great ways to socialize if your son invites a group of friends over, and they can be fun to watch and enjoy. They can also provide a welcome escape from reality. These are all reasons that an appropriate amount of television or movies is fine. Try to find shows that reflect your family's values or interests. This will help you view televisions and movies as friend and not foe.

By watching television with your son, you have the opportunity to get him to open up and talk to him about what he's watching. If you watch with your son, you will know what he's watching and he will know you're watching too. Sometimes it can also be less intimidating to talk when it isn't just you and your son staring at each other.

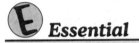 **Essential**

To limit the amount of time your son spends in front of a computer or television screen, set a cap on screen time in your home. Figure out a plan for how to count homework time in front of a screen—if you allow it at all.

While you can't watch everything he watches, you can get a good sense of what his tastes may be. You can get a sense for a particular television series and feel more comfortable with him watching it. The same is true of books that have been made into movies. Some parents feel that they can be a bit more lenient about movie violence if their son has first read the book. Take Harry Potter for example. It's violent, but many kids have already read the books and formed the images in their minds.

Older teens like more graphic movies, and even some of those can have redeeming values. For example, there is a lot of violence in the *Pirates of the Caribbean* movies, and Captain Jack Sparrow is quite the pirate; however, he still manages to do the right thing when the time calls for it. In the end, it is your job as a parent to decide what is appropriate for your son. You can also talk to other parents who share your beliefs when making this decision.

Music and Music Videos

Music is an important part of being a teenager. There are MP3s, CDs, and radio stations, bands who tour and bands who don't, and no matter what they sound like to you, they all mean something to your son. The question lies in where you and your values fit in with the music your son listens to.

The Importance of Music

Music helps your teen find his identity. It can also be something that helps him identify with other teens his age. Music, and especially lyrics, can help define social and cultural interests.

Because music is so significant to your son, it is very important to know what he is listening to on a daily basis. Ask him to share some music with you or let him choose the radio stations when you drive somewhere together. This can be a good way to talk and yet show him you are interested in what his music is about. Don't worry if it's not your style or if you don't like it; he doesn't really expect you to, but it shows him that you care.

When to Worry about Music

Just because music is important to your son does not mean you should give him complete and free rein on the music he listens to every day. Most teens identify with the lyrics. Typically they are drawn to lyrics and music that concern the struggles in their own lives—growing up, love, cars, dating, and other teen topics. This is a healthy thing for your son—to a point.

The problem is when song lyrics contain words and ideas that are racist, sexist, or pro-violence. Popular songs feature lyrics about gang violence and glorify drugs, rape, and other dangerous topics. Teens who are drawn to violent music and who exhibit anti-social or depressed behavior are at a greater risk for problems, including drug and alcohol abuse and other risky behaviors. Listen to your son's music with him. If his choices are illegal in nature, nix them, but be careful when doing this.

Music Videos

Music videos are also an issue for most families. When MTV started in the early 1980s, the videos were novel, and they very quickly became the coolest thing on television. Today, music videos are available on the Internet and on television.

Music videos can link disturbing images to the lyrics. Since many of the lyrics are garbled, the pictures are what may stay with your son. The videos can be overly sexual or violent, and music videos aren't rated like movies. You should sit down to watch television and watch the music videos just as you would any other program. Be sure to talk to your son about what he is seeing. Tell him what you find wrong with the video. Ask him questions and see what his responses are.

Video Games

Kids love video games. They are an easy form of entertainment and an outlet to relieve frustrations. While video games can be fun and help kids relax, they are also not necessarily the best thing for your son, partly because of the time spent on them and partly because of the high levels of violence in many of the games.

E *Essential*

There are ratings for television, movies, music, and video games. The American Academy of Pediatrics has a Web site that explains the ratings for parents at *www.aap.org/family/ ratingsgame.htm.*

Video-Game Violence

The American Psychological Association (APA) released a news report on some recent research that found that playing violent video games like Doom or Mortal Combat can increase teenagers' feelings of aggressiveness. This held true in the laboratory setting as well as in real life.

Characters in these games are very vivid. They are fully digitized human beings that require your son to associate with them in order to play—and playing involves shooting and killing. This can be even more harmful than the violence on television or in the movies because your son has to take action and is not merely watching.

Finding a Happy Balance

Video games are not totally horrible. Some video games teach typing or work on certain skills, including academic skills. Some teachers use videos as a part of an educational task.

As with anything, the key is control. As the parent, you need to decide which games your son is allowed to play and how long he is allowed to play them. Many electronics stores have games available for customers to test. This might be a nice field trip to have with your son, and it would give you a chance to see the games he is drawn to and check out the ratings for yourself.

 Fact

Kids who spend a lot of time playing video games usually spend less time on physical activity. There are also games that try to include movement, like the Dance Dance Revolution games and the Nintendo Wii.

The Internet

The Internet is a valuable resource for your son. It literally gives him the world at his fingertips. The key is to find out how to best use the Internet for your son and to teach him the responsibility in relation to it.

Great Uses for the Internet

The Internet is a great place for your son to learn. He can scout out potential colleges, do research for school papers, and communicate with his teachers and friends.

You can also have your son show you some interesting things on the Internet. Try sitting down with your son. Show him some of the neat things you've found on the Net and tools that you use. Then ask that he show you what he enjoys doing on the Internet as well.

Internet Warnings

While the Internet has a large capacity for good, there is a dark side. Keeping your son safe reaches far beyond teaching him proper ergonomics.

E Alert

Teens are vulnerable to Internet predators. The more involved you are with your son and the computer, the less likely this is to happen. Your son wants someone to pay attention to him; it can be you or it can be a "friendly" Internet pervert.

Establish rules for Internet usage and be sure your son knows them and any consequences for disobeying them. Your rules should also include a time limit and what he is allowed and not allowed to do. Install blocking software to prevent him from going to sites that aren't appropriate. Today's parents have a tough time being as computer savvy as their kids, who may be quite adept at bypassing blocking software. Parents still need to supervise their teens' Internet use. Do not allow your son to have a computer in his bedroom or another place where you cannot monitor it.

Talk to your son about the dangers of the Internet. He needs to understand that posting personal information, however innocuous it may seem, is a bad idea. He needs to understand about Internet predators and even just mean-spirited people. In short, your expertise is required for a positive Net experience.

Chapter 12

Risky Business

Children are exposed to drugs all the time. Most of these we don't even consider, such as the prescription drugs in our homes. Kids also see people socially drinking or smoking. Many of the people they see using drugs are people they trust and respect. Your job as a parent is to teach your son about drug use and abuse. This is not an easy task.

Tobacco: Chew, Snuff, and Cigarettes

Tobacco is one of the most accepted social drugs. Seeing posters of lungs blackened by cigarettes and the oral cancers caused by smokeless tobacco doesn't stop teens from using these products in an effort to be cool or rebel. Nicotine is highly addictive, and what may start as innocent experimentation may lead to a problem your son can't deal with alone.

Who Is Smoking?

In 2005, the Youth Risk Behavior Surveillance System (YRBSS) of the Centers for Disease Control and Prevention

showed that 54.3 percent of students had tried smoking cigarettes. About 25.6 percent of these teens smoked before the
age of thirteen. Another 8 percent tried smokeless tobacco,
while 14 percent smoked cigars.

Essential

If you are a smoker, consider quitting. Share the struggles of
quitting with your son and ask for his support. You can try
many programs available through hospitals, doctors, and
associations.

As a parent, let your son know straight up that you consider
chew, snuff, and cigarettes to be drugs. He should know the
consequences for using drugs. Then you have to enforce the
rules if you find your son has broken them.

Some studies show that adolescent boys who are involved
in sports are less likely to use tobacco products than teens
who aren't athletic. Regardless, your son should know how
tobacco products affect his body.

How to Help Your Son Quit

If your son has already started smoking, help him quit.
Smoking is highly addictive, and the sooner he quits, the better. It is important that your son know the following effects of
smoking on his body:

- Decrease in the rate of lung growth and function
- Drop in athletic endurance and performance

- Increased risk of respiratory illnesses
- Increased risk for the development of lung cancer
- Greater likelihood of becoming ill and staying ill
- Decrease in heart function
- Decrease in sense of taste and smell
- Increase in tooth decay and number of cavities
- Decrease in certain hormone levels

Among adult smokers, 90 percent started smoking before they were eighteen years old. If you can help your son not start smoking, you can increase the probability that he will lead a smoke-free life.

 *E-Fact*

Even if your son does not personally smoke, he may be around others who do smoke. Let him know he has the right and responsibility to protect his body from the more than forty-three carcinogens in cigarette smoke.

Smokeless tobaccos (chew and snuff) are also dangerous, causing such problems as periodontal disease, high blood pressure, and oral cancer. Like smoking, they can be extremely difficult to quit. Your son will need your support. Consider helping him find a program designed specifically for teens, no matter which type of tobacco he uses. You may want to talk to your health care provider about ways to deal with the oral fixations that go along with snuff, chew, or smokeless tobacco.

Alcohol

Teenagers are bombarded with images of alcohol use, almost all of them associating drinking with good times. Alcohol is widely available, and it is one of the most abused drugs among adolescents.

How Bad Is the Problem?

By the age of eighteen, 80 to 90 percent of teens have tried alcohol. The average age to start drinking has dropped from fourteen to twelve in recent years, and an estimated 4.6 million teens between the ages of fourteen and seventeen have significant alcohol problems. Motor vehicle accidents are the leading cause of death for teenagers, and as many as one-third of fatal crashes involve alcohol. Alcohol is also a factor in adolescent depression, poor performance in school, sexual activity, date rape, assaults, accidental deaths, and even homicide.

Alcohol is easy for teens to get their hands on. Many establishments will sell to minors, and some children know someone of legal drinking age who will obtain it for them. Some teens steal alcohol from their own homes, and some parents give their children alcohol because they feel it is safer than having their children obtain it by other means.

Alcohol is a central nervous system depressant. Even in small quantities, alcohol can impair judgment and coordination. Aggressiveness can be seen even with low amounts of alcohol; this is a bad combination for the already hormonally charged teens. At higher amounts, alcohol can impair mental functioning, including the ability to remember information.

Drinking too much can lead to alcohol poisoning, which can cause irreversible brain damage or death.

Essential

Filled with anime-like drawings and tons of information on alcohol and peer pressure, *www.thecoolspot.gov* is a great site for your son. It has quizzes and other fun and interactive tools for him, including role-playing scenes for him to judge.

What Can You Do?

The first thing you should do as a parent is work toward prevention. Teach your son about the dangers of alcohol. Explain to him the reasons that there are limits on who can drink. You should also teach him how to say no to alcohol and let him know he can call you for a ride with no fear of repercussions if his ride becomes drunk.

You should also look for signs of alcohol use and abuse in your son. Signs include:

- Smelling of alcohol
- Missing alcohol at home
- Problems at school
- A new crowd of friends
- Friends with a history of alcohol use/abuse
- Increase in sleeping/decrease in energy
- Slurred speech and disorientation
- Moodiness
- Bloodshot eyes

If your son gets alcohol poisoning, seek medical attention immediately. Follow up with psychological help. If you suspect your teen is drinking alcohol, talk to him about it. Do not wait for proof to present itself, but do not accuse your son of drinking if you aren't sure. Restate your rules and the consequences, open up a discussion on alcohol, and keep an eye on him.

 Fact

Drinking large quantities at one time is known as binge drinking. This is a huge problem on university campuses and has resulted in deaths from both alcohol poisoning and accidents. Be sure your son knows about the dangers of binge drinking.

Inhalants

Teens inhale the fumes from ordinary products to get high. Inhalants are known by many names, including hippie crack, huff, Medusa, moon gas, Oz, airblast, bang, discorama, and poor man's pot.

Why Inhaling Is Bad

Inhalants are typical items found in your house. Frequent offenders include nail polish remover, permanent markers, spray paint, whipped cream, adhesives, paint thinner, typewriter correction fluid, deodorants, lighter fluid, aerosol cans, cooking spray, household cleaners, and even gasoline. Inhaling is the deliberate sniffing of these products.

Essential

Inhalant.org has some tools for parents, including talking points and warning signs. It has message boards and information on prevention of inhalant abuse as well as information designed for kids and teens.

Some teens soak their clothing and smell the products all day, while others sniff painted fingernails or other objects, including notebooks, pens, and other personal items. Some teens place products in a bag and then inhale directly from the bag; this is known as bagging.

Inhalants starve the body of oxygen, causing a high. The dangers of inhalants are largely ignored by teens, who think, "How dangerous can it be? It's whipped cream—we eat it." Inhalants can cause loss of muscle control, damage to major organs, brain damage, and death. Inhalants can kill the very first time they are used; such deaths usually result from cardiac issues related to the overworking of the heart muscle.

According to a 2005 report from the Centers for Disease Control and Prevention, 12.4 percent of teens have tried inhalants. Inhalants are easy to come by and are inexpensive if purchased, unlike many other drugs.

How Do I Know If My Teen Is Doing Inhalants?

Inhalants can be very scary for parents because they are so readily available. There are some signs of inhalant abuse that may be helpful to look for, including the following:

- Empty cans of items with nitrous oxide, like whipped cream
- Hidden cans of spray paint or solvent (full or empty)
- Poor coordination
- Acting drunk or disoriented
- Paint or chemical stains on clothes or rags
- Clothes soaked in chemicals
- Painted nails
- Sniffing glue, pens, or markers
- Sores in the nose or mouth
- Red, weepy eyes

Inhalants, tobacco, and alcohol can all serve as gateway drugs. Adolescents try these drugs before moving along to illegal drugs that are harder to obtain.

Steroids

Anabolic steroids (also known as roids or juice) are related to testosterone, a male hormone. While they are technically legal, there are very few prescriptions written for anabolic steroids. They are very different from other steroid medications commonly prescribed for conditions like asthma.

Why Use Steroids?

Students who want to bulk up or build muscle may turn to steroids. Abuse is not uncommon among teen athletes. Steroids can help them increase muscle mass and body weight. This gives them more endurance and strength, which are assets on the playing field—but performance-enhancing drugs are banned from organized competition.

Ⓔ *Essential*

The National Institute on Drug Abuse runs a Web site dedicated to steroid abuse at *www.steroidabuse.org*. Here you can find the latest research on steroid abuse as well as helpful tips for parents.

Steroids can be taken orally or injected. Injecting may put your son at an increased risk of contracting hepatitis or HIV/AIDS because many teens share needles. Many adolescents will cycle these drugs rather than take them continually. Teens may also use different steroids to maximize the benefits and offset the long-term health effects, which include:

- Increased blood pressure
- Jaundice
- Fluid retention
- Increases in acne
- Heart problems
- Stroke
- Cancer
- Liver problems
- Heart attacks
- Sterility
- Impotence
- Slowing of growth that may permanently affect height

Is My Son Taking Steroids?

Every teen needs to know about the risks of steroid abuse. That said, there are some teen populations that are more at risk, including athletes. Some boys who are smaller in stature or are picked on because of their height may also be tempted by steroids.

Steroids have many side effects. Those around your son would notice many of these side effects. These changes can alert you to the fact that your son may be abusing anabolic steroids:

- Increase in aggression (physical and psychological)
- Increase in agitation and irritability
- Increase or onset of paranoia
- Increase in jealousy
- Depression
- Delusions

If you notice any of these signs or suspect your son is using anabolic steroids, make an appointment with your son's health care practitioner.

Abusing Legal Drugs

The common perception of drugs focuses on illegal substances sold on street corners or in alleys. However, many teens abuse drugs they find in their own homes.

What Drugs Are Abused?

While some drugs are more susceptible to abuse, any drug can be abused. About 4 million children ages twelve and over use prescription drugs for nonmedical reasons. While girls may be more likely to misuse prescription drugs, boys do their fair share.

 Alert

> If your son is taking medications that were prescribed by a medical care provider for a specific problem, the risk of addiction is very low. However, you should warn your son about sharing or selling his medications. You should also talk to his provider about his risks of abuse and make sure your son goes in for regular checkups.

You should be mindful of pain medications (Oxycontin, Vicodin, Percocet, Tylenol 3, and so forth); medications used to treat attention deficit/hyperactivity disorder (such as Ritalin); and medications used to treat anxiety (such as Valium and Xanax).

Cough Syrup and Other Household Items

You may remember how, as a young child, your son resisted taking cough medicine and you had to wrestle with him to force it down his throat. For teens, chugging cough syrup or swallowing large numbers of pills is an easy way to get high. Cough syrups fall into two main categories: those with codeine (code named AC/DC, Barr) and those with dextromethorphan (DXM; slang terms include Robo, Robo tripping, Tussin, Dex). The short-term side effects include:

- Nausea and/or vomiting
- Sweating
- Abdominal pain
- Hyperactivity
- Hallucinations
- Increase in blood pressure
- Seizures
- Changes in heartbeat

 *E-Alert*

Many teens mix DXM with other drugs. Some teens will use DXM to coat marijuana joints or dilute it with alcoholic drinks to negate the nasty flavor. You may also hear that some teens are using ecstasy with DXM as well.

In pill form, teens also ingest other chemicals meant to alleviate cold/cough symptoms, including acetaminophen and/or antihistamines. Some of these combinations can cause liver damage, in addition to the other dangers of cough syrup abuse, which include:

- Passing out
- Hemorrhaging in the brain

- Permanent brain damage
- Stroke

Parents often overlook seemingly innocuous over-the-counter medications, but make sure you talk to your son about drug abuse and the potential dangers to his health.

Illegal drugs

Parents have always feared illegal drugs, and that fear is well founded. Having good, honest conversations with your son can help make all the difference in the world. Knowing the basics about the drugs that are popular in your area is important to helping prevent drug use in your child.

Marijuana

Marijuana is a drug that can be smoked or ingested. It is the most commonly used illegal drug in the United States. What gives marijuana (also known as cannabis, MJ, Mary Jane, and weed) its power is the chemical tetrahydrocannabinol (THC).

E *Fact*

Some states have legalized the use of marijuana for medical purposes. The difference is that medicinal marijuana use is overseen by doctors and is not potentially tainted the way street drugs can be.

Marijuana makes users feel euphoric yet laid-back. Marijuana is also known to heighten sensory experiences. Physically, a person's heart rate and appetite increase. Short-term memory, motivation, and thinking can also be adversely affected. There is also the potential for lung damage, including lung cancer. Long-term users are more likely to drop out of school, have low sperm count, and feel like marijuana is their sole purpose for existing.

Cocaine

Cocaine is a truly frightening drug. It is derived from the coca bush in South America and acts as a stimulant. It comes in two forms, cocaine and crack cocaine. Cocaine is a white powder that is mixed or cut with other powdered substances including talcum powder, infant formula (artificial baby milk), corn starch, or even other drugs. The concentration of cocaine in a given batch can vary widely. In this form, cocaine can be snorted, freebased (smoked), and mainlined (injected). Crack cocaine, a potent form of cocaine, in soft rock form, is more readily available and less expensive, making it a favorite among teens. This highly addictive form of cocaine is ready to smoke.

 Alert

Cocaine has the potential to be tainted with other drugs that the user doesn't know about. Other drugs are used to increase the volume of the drug or its effects. This can have deadly consequences.

Users feel wildly euphoric and high. They get a rush. The problem is that the rush doesn't last very long—about five to thirty minutes. After that, the user feels a sense of deep depression. Cocaine is highly addictive, and a single use can cause a person to become physically addicted. Cocaine can cause:

- Dilated pupils
- Increase blood pressure
- Rise in body temperature
- Increased rate of breathing
- Racing heart
- Runny nose (short-term use) or sores in the nasal passages (long-term use)

Someone on cocaine can become violent and aggressive. Users can also suffer from convulsions, heart attack, stroke, changes in the heartbeat, respiratory depression, and lack of oxygen to vital organs. Mainlining or injecting cocaine can also expose your son to the risks for hepatitis, HIV/AIDS, and other diseases.

Amphetamines

This class of stimulants is more readily available and less expensive than cocaine. Because the amphetamines work on the central nervous system, the user will feel wide awake and alert. Students take these drugs to help them prepare for tests or to stay awake for long projects. Amphetamines can be ingested, injected, snorted, or smoked.

Fact

A 2005 report by the Centers for Disease Control and Prevention found 6.2 percent of high school students responded they had used methamphetamines during their lifetime. This number was down from 2003 and 2001.

Teens who use methamphetamines may exhibit aggressive behavior and many of the same side effects as with cocaine, including headache, anxiety, and dizziness. Amphetamines can leave the user feeling high for hours, compared to cocaine's short-lived high.

Sedatives

Sedatives work much like alcohol on the central nervous system. They can make the user feel less anxious, and calm. They can also impair muscular control and make the user slur his speech or feel drowsy. Many of these drugs are legal but misused, as when taken by someone other than the person for whom they were prescribed.

Designer or Club Drugs

This class of drugs includes:

- LSD (lysergic acid diethylamide)
- PCP (phencyclidine)
- Ketamine
- Mescaline
- MDMA/Ecstacy (methylenedioxymethamphetamine)

These drugs are ingested or smoked to produce euphoric feelings. They are hallucinogens. One place your teen may find these is at an all-night party or rave where music and lights are combined with drugs and dancing to produce a psychedelic experience.

 Alert

Your son may try to take something known as Herbal Ecstasy. It creates a heightened sense of alertness that causes stress. It is found in music shops and on the counters at many convenience stores. Your son needs to understand why this is dangerous, despite being legal.

Date Rape Drugs

While Rohypnol (roofies) is the most heard of in this category, there are other drugs that can be used as well, including GHB (gamma hydroxybutyric acid). These drugs are used to relax the user, who typically is unaware that he or she has been drugged. Date rape drugs also prevent the person who was drugged from remembering what happened.

These drugs can easily be slipped into drinks. Since they are colorless and odorless, they can't be detected. Hoffmann-LaRoche Inc., the manufacturer of Rohypnol, is developing their drug to change colors and become clumpy in liquids to help combat this problem. Teens can order this drug over the Internet from other countries using only a credit card.

Defining the Rules

It is imperative that you talk to your son about drugs. According to the National Center on Addiction and Substance Abuse at Columbia University, a recent survey of middle and high school students showed that half the children had never had a talk about drugs with their parents. It is your responsibility to talk to your son, and communication is the best tool you have to prevent drug use.

Preventing Drug Use

Drug abuse is also not something your child simply decides to do. Most teens think they will just try a drug once for fun to see what the hype is about. They don't realize that there is a very slippery slope that quickly leads to abuse and addiction. Even perfect parents and perfect teens can fall victim to drug abuse.

 Fact

Columbia University's Center on Addiction and Substance Abuse reported a third of teens and nearly half of the seventeen-year-olds surveyed had attended a party where the parents were present while the teens abused a variety of drugs.

Before you talk to your son, it is important that you know your drugs facts. There are plenty of places to get information on drugs. You can try Web sites, and books are good sources of information. This will help show you know what you are talking about. It will also give you the ability to answer questions your son may ask about drug use.

When you feel more confident, talk to your son. Find a time and place you can sit down and talk without being interrupted. You should have plenty of time available. While this big talk will be a great start, it is not the end. You should take every chance you have to reinforce your position with your son. Find times to slip in facts or questions about drug use. This will keep you both on your toes.

Household Rules about Drugs

Firm rules about drug use are imperative. You and your son should both know the rules and the consequences for breaking them. If needed, you must enforce the rules with no exceptions.

Ⓔ *Essential*

Be sure the parents of your son's friends have similar rules about drugs and alcohol. Be sure they are not enabling kids to drink or do drugs in their home. Do not hesitate to nix your son's plans if they seem worrisome.

There should be one main rule in your family: Drugs are not to ever be used. Ever. Period. Your son should not allow his friends to use drugs in his presence. The consequences should be appropriate for the violation. If your son has been caught drinking or taking drugs, it may be inappropriate for him to use the car, even if the car was not a part of the original infraction. You should also avoid adding new consequences for infractions—stick to the original plan.

When to Get Professional Help

No parent wants to find out their son is using drugs. That said, the reality is that even if you do everything correctly, your son may still use drugs. He may even become dependent on drugs or suffer other harmful side effects.

Signs Your Son Needs Help

The typical behavior of teens can feel very bewildering. Drug use might not be the only cause of some of the signs your son needs help. These signs can include:

- Sudden changes in personality
- Marked increase in irresponsible behavior
- Change in personal appearance (clothing or hygiene)
- Secretive behavior
- Decrease in interest in hobbies
- Poor grades
- Irrational or rebellious behavior
- Change in friends
- Increase in music or literature that is pro-drug
- Drug paraphernalia
- Physical signs of drug abuse or use

Remember that some of these signs may be normal behavior for your son. The difference in a child who needs help is that the signs are not short-lived. If after a few days your son is still exhibiting these signs, it's time to get help. It may or may not be drugs, but he still needs professional help.

Your Son Is Caught

If you think your son is taking drugs, don't panic. That will actually cause more problems. If you think he is currently under the influence of drugs, don't argue or confront him; it may cause a violent reaction. If you find your son unconscious, call 9-1-1 immediately. Start applying first aid if he needs it. If he is breathing, simply turn him on his side and wait. Try to figure out what he took, when, and with whom. Ask those around him or people he was recently with.

Wait until your son sobers up to talk to him. He may try to lie or make excuses, but it is important for you to be firm and calm. If this is a first offense, simply invoke the rules previously put into place and the punishments attached to them. If the drug use becomes a repeated problem, seek help from a professional.

Types of Help Available

Sometimes the hardest thing for a parent to do is to ask for outside help. Once you have determined that your son has a problem that he needs to seek treatment for, you need to act confidently and swiftly to minimize the damage.

Finding a Therapist

One of the first steps may be to find a local therapist who can help your son. It should be someone who has experience working with teens because this is a specialized area. There are many different types of practitioners available. The therapist you choose may be a psychiatrist, psychologist, a nurse practitioner with an advanced nursing degree, or a social worker.

E) *Essential*

Your insurance may dictate what practitioner you see. Be sure to check with both your insurance and the practitioner to review their policies. Some insurance requires special authorization for certain treatments for substance abuse.

If you don't know where to start in finding help for your son, turn to others you trust. This might be your son's health care provider, the school counselor, or even your own health care provider. You can also look at the list provided by your insurance company or by a teen agency in town. Armed with a list, you should interview each person. Questions should include:

- Licensure or credentials
- Areas of practice expertise
- Experience with the topic and age group
- Office policies including hours, payments, backup practitioners, and fees
- Types of therapy used

In-Patient Facilities

If your son is in very bad medical shape or is at risk of hurting himself or others, hospitalization may be required.

This may be at a medical facility, a psychiatric facility, or a center that specializes in drug and alcohol treatment. Once in the hospital he will receive individual and group therapy as well as any medical care or tests needed. Typically, hospitalization lasts only a week or two, until your son is stable. From there he may be referred to a partial hospital program or a day program.

Fact

Your son's practitioner may be obligated to keep certain matters confidential, which means not even you can have access to them. This should be explained ahead of time.

A day program is one where your son attends counseling and therapy in an intense program, but only during the day. This is not as severe as inpatient treatment, but it is still intense. He may have certain restrictions at home, for he will be there in the evenings and during the weekends.

When your son graduates from a day program, he will still require therapy for the long term. Consider having him continue the therapy through his teen years and into college. College is another big period of adjustment, and therapy is a protective mechanism to help him prevent reverting back to his old habits.

Chapter 13

Dating and Sexuality

Few things strike fear in the heart of the parent of a teen-aged boy as much as the thought of dating, sex, and sexuality. You may worry about having "the talk" with your son. You may fear the day he says he wants to date someone. As a parent, you have the responsibility to talk to your son about these issues, and the best way to handle them is with respect, authority, and compassion.

Having "The Talk"

Parents often worry about having to talk about sex and sexuality with their child. The good news is that there are a great many more resources available to parents today than there were in our own parents' generation. While the information is readily available, it can also feel overwhelming at times. The basics are always a really great place to start.

Not a Once-in-a-Lifetime Event

You should look at the topic of sexuality as a series of discussions, rather than one lengthy conversation. There are many resources available for having these discussions. Some of the resources available are for teens and some are for parents. Talk to other parents to see what they recommend. You may also get a good recommendation from your son's health care provider.

 **Essential**

Teen boys may try to avoid checkups with the doctor, even when the doctor is not a pediatrician. The reason? It's not cool. Talk to your son about the importance of checkups, and be sure he gets his annual checkups throughout his teen years.

Questions: What Is Your Son Asking?

It is natural for children to have questions beginning at a very early age. Make sure you understand the question before you launch into an explanation. When your son asks, "What is birth control?" he may not be asking where to buy condoms, but simply for the definition of the phrase. It's easy to scare teens with too much information.

The opposite is also true. Parents can certainly provide too little information. This means that your resourceful teen son will find the information through his own sources. The bad news here is that these sources may be inaccurate and lack your values and judgment. Even though the questions may be frightening for your son and uncomfortable for you both, do not hesitate to talk to your son.

 Fact

Testicular cancer is most common between the ages of fifteen and thirty-nine. Your son needs to know how to perform a testicular self-exam. You can get brochures on how to perform a TSE from your health care provider or online.

Circumcision may become a question at this point. Some boys are and some boys aren't. They may begin to notice the differences about now. If you haven't discussed your decisions regarding circumcision before, now is an appropriate time. Be sure to discuss the proper care of his penis and penile health in general.

What to Do When He's Not Talking

If your son is not coming to you with questions, take the initiative. A good subject to start with is simply changes in his body, preferably before they happen. Discussing what puberty can do to his mind and body will help prepare him for the changes and give you the chance to start the conversation on a safe note.

From this point, you can move on to other topics. Remember that some issues will be more comfortable than others. Try to start with what you are comfortable with. Some possible topics to discuss with your teen son include, but are not limited to:

- Puberty
- The male body
- The female body
- The mechanics of sex
- Emotions and sex
- Birth control
- Pregnancy
- Sexually transmitted diseases (STDs)
- Alternatives to sex

 Fact

According to the Centers for Disease Control and Prevention, 62 percent of the HIV/AIDS diagnoses between 2001 and 2004 were for young men between the ages of thirteen and twenty-four. This is a huge problem and something that you cannot ignore.

How to Talk to Your Son

There is a right time to talk to your son and many bad times. Do not start a conversation in front of his friends or siblings. Try to find a time that you are both in a relatively good mood.

Set the ground rules for the discussion. Remind him that you are there to help him and admit when you do not know something. Just let him know that you will find out the answers to his questions. As long as you are honest and open, you will establish a solid foundation with your son. Remember, he hasn't done this before either.

The only mistake you can make is not talking to him and letting him attempt to figure matters out for himself; this will increase the possibility that he will find incorrect information or jump to incorrect conclusions. If you find that you simply have trouble talking to your son, try to find someone to role-play with you.

Ⓔ *Essential*

Using instant messaging or e-mail may be a good trick if he seems incredibly embarrassed or if you are. This may help him be more open and honest. This should not be how all conversations are held, however, as it may convey the belief that sexuality is something to be embarrassed about.

Sex Versus Sexuality

One of your jobs as a parent is to prepare your son to be a healthy sexual human being. This is a complex matter, involving many concepts from the physical to the mental to the emotional. As a teen, your son may find it difficult to integrate all of this information, which is where parents come in.

Sexuality encompasses the whole body and mind, including the genitals, but it is more about the giving and receiving of pleasure than the mere act of sex.

A person's sexuality is largely affected by surroundings, and parents often influence a teenager's surroundings. Other factors that can influence sexuality include values, attitudes, behaviors, physical appearance, and spiritual beliefs.

Sexual Orientation

Sexual orientation relates to whom you find attractive and wish to have sexual relationships with. Most people refer to this as heterosexuality, homosexuality, or bisexuality. The teenage years are a time when many boys will question their sexual orientation, no matter what it is. Your response is critical to helping your son grow.

Gay Teens

Labeling teen sexuality is difficult, as some young teen boys may occasionally feel attracted to other males, yet not be homosexual. Others know they are gay. A 1995 Massachusetts Youth Risk Behavior Survey found that 2.5 percent of youth self-identified as gay, lesbian, or bisexual. Your son's disclosure can be traumatic for you, and it is common for parents to feel a sense of loss when they learn their son is gay. You may even go through Dr. Kubler-Ross's stages of denial, anger, bargaining, depression, and, finally, acceptance.

 Alert

If your son is gay, you are not alone! There are other parents who can help you sort through your questions. Parents, Family, and Friends of Lesbians and Gays (*www.pflag.org*) is one such organization with many tools to help you and your son.

Acceptance is critical, as your son needs your love and recognition to help him succeed in a society that can be very cruel to him because of his sexual orientation. He may face problems such as anti-gay harassment and violence. Gay teens also have a higher risk of suicide, and they are at risk for HIV and eating disorders. Therefore, your son needs to know that you will be there for him unconditionally. For help on how to talk to your son, talk to your health care provider or go to *www.keepingkidshealthy.com* for a variety of resources on raising a gay teen.

You must identify your own feelings and deal with them, but the most important thing for you to do immediately is to confirm to your son that you love him. Tell him that nothing that he can ever do or say will change the way you feel about him. He needs to hear this from you now and often in the future, as do all children.

Being Gay Is Not a Choice

Homosexuality involves an intricate mixture of biological, genetic, and social factors. Being gay is not a choice, nor is it anyone's fault, least of all your son's.

Some young men are confused about their sexuality. They may have strong feelings toward other young men, but also like young women. Sometimes this is a natural part of growing up and dealing with hormones. The huge hormonal fluctuations can make your son attracted to many people. This may or may not mean he is gay, and he will figure out his sexual orientation in time.

It is important that you not try to change your son. Reparative therapy can be very harmful and will not "cure" homosexuality. However, therapy with a trained and skilled therapist who has experience with gay teens can help your son through a confusing and difficult time. Gay teens are more likely to commit suicide and be depressed than other teens. With your support and the professional support that you find, your son has a much better chance of not becoming one of those statistics. Talk to your son about sex and about special problems he may face, like discrimination.

Masturbation

The topic of self-love is the punch line of many hysterical teen movies and urban legends. Since the beginning of time, people have circulated myths about masturbation—that it causes blindness or mental derangement. The subject needs to be brought up delicately.

Masturbation Is Normal

You probably noticed that your son liked to put his hand on his penis, even as a baby. As soon as he figured out where it was, his hand was there. Many parents attest that diapers didn't even contain their son's desires. While masturbation starts as something without a purpose other than feeling good, once puberty hits, there is a whole new light to masturbation—sexual release.

Your son may think about masturbation but never do it, or he may think about masturbation and masturbate multiple times a day. These are both normal variations. The only thing wrong with masturbation is the psychological harm it could cause if your son were to feel guilty about it.

Talking about Masturbation

The important thing to remember is that masturbation is normal. But it can be frightening for your son if you do not teach him early enough in life that masturbation is normal and healthy. It is important to tell him that it is nothing to be ashamed of or worried about. You also need to provide him with answers to his questions and information about where he can turn should he have more questions.

 Fact

Your son may experience nocturnal emissions or wet dreams—spontaneous discharge of seminal fluid from his penis. The embarrassment of wet sheets and not quite knowing what's going on may inspire him to do a load of laundry.

To start a conversation about masturbation, you might try to bring up the topic of hygiene. This can start as a very casual chat. Talk to him about the proper way to clean and care for his penis and scrotum. Explain to him that erections happen. He should already know what an erection is and why it happens. During his adolescence, he will have more frequent erections, sometimes for no apparent reason. Let the conversation move on from there.

You may want to buy him a book about body changes that includes information on masturbation. You can also help him find some appropriate Web sites that you have screened. The most important part is that he has a person, preferably a parent, to talk to about this topic.

Talking to your son about masturbation may include dispelling myths. For example, if someone has told your son that masturbation will make him blind and he has recently experienced visual changes, which are normal as the body grows in puberty, he may be worried that his new need for glasses results from his newest hobby.

E-Fact

Erections are a fact of life. Your son may experience them anywhere and for any reason. Try to help him figure out how to deal with them, including what to say when a teacher asks him to stand up in class while an erection is raging.

Dating Responsibly

Dating is a wide-open topic. It involves so many of the same topics as the discussion of responsibility: curfews and boundaries, sex and sexuality.

Your Job as Parent of a Son Who Dates

Teach your son how to interact with his date's parents. Many parents may ask to meet him before saying "yes" to the date. Coach him on shaking hands and maintaining appropriate eye contact.

Discuss the art of small talk. While it is helpful for him to be able to converse with his date's parents, it is also quite useful for those awkward moments during a date.

Sex

Sex is not a four-letter word. Your son needs to learn the joys and responsibilities of relationships. He needs to know how you feel about sex and in what type of relationships you believe sex is appropriate.

If you rely on television and movies to give you an accurate picture of modern teens and sex, chances are you'll feel pretty bleak. Yes, teens have sex. No, not all teens have sex. If you prefer that your son stay off the sex bandwagon, then make sure you talk to him about your feelings.

Essential

Luckily, many dates are group dates, which means individuals usually pay for themselves. However, you need to talk to your son about how to handle the bill when there are only two people at a table.

As a parent, you need to watch what you say about sex. It is really easy to scare teenagers into believing sex is awful and horrible. Make sure your son understands the gravity of sex and its potential consequences—both emotional and physical—but let him know that it is an exceptional experience given the right environment and relationship.

Your son is more likely to have faith and trust you if you do not rely solely on scare tactics to describe sex. This also leaves the door open for more discussions on the topic. If he knows you are understanding about sex, he will be more likely to ask you questions and be honest with you. This gives you more power as a parent to be there for him and to help shape his attitudes about sex.

Teen Pregnancy

As the parent of a boy you have probably not given a lot of thought to teen pregnancy. This is fairly common among the parents of boys because it does not affect them, right? Wrong.

Teen pregnancy is a two-way street. Your son needs to know that he cannot assume birth control is the woman's job. He must understand that a condom is a good thing; even if he is having sex with someone who is taking oral contraceptives, a condom will help prevent some STDs. Your son is just as responsible as the girl is if a pregnancy occurs. To prevent your son from getting someone pregnant, you first need to talk to him about what causes pregnancy and how to prevent it.

Study after study shows that abstinence-only education is not effective in reducing the rates of teen pregnancy. Your son must know about birth control as well.

Girlfriends

Ah, girlfriends. Yes, your son may choose to date someone exclusively. This is still called a girlfriend, but outdated terms like going steady have definitely gone the way of the woolly mammoth. If your son chooses to see someone in this fashion, the rules change.

What Is a Girlfriend?

Be sure to clarify with your son how he defines the term "girlfriend." While it may mean an exclusive relationship, it may also mean something else. He can give you the answers you're looking for on the meaning of this relationship.

You need to talk to him about whether or not the girl-friend knows she is in an exclusive relationship. Is this something they have decided on together, or something your son assumes because they have gone out for a certain period of time? Making sure that he clarifies this information can help save hurt feelings down the road.

My Son Is Dating **Who?!**

It can happen that your son is dating someone you don't like. Your temptation may be to do everything you can within your power to dissolve the relationship, even to the point of forbidding them to see each other. This only sets you up for a very negative situation and allows him to rationalize ignoring you and hiding information from you. Basically, by taking this type of stance, you've set yourself up to be completely left out of the loop.

 Fact

Asking a girl out can be really scary for your son. Give him advice on how to ask someone out before he has to face it alone. Remind him to be polite, ask in private, and show self-confidence.

You will probably have better luck by trying to talk to him about what is right about the relationship to him. This opens up the lines of communication. He may then be more willing to talk to you about what is going on with his girlfriend.

Friends Who Are Girls

Your son may have relationships with girls who he claims are only friends. Do not jump to conclusions and assume he is not telling the truth. There are plenty of boy/girl friendships that are purely friendships.

Positive Relationships

The good news about your son having friends who are girls is that it enables him to have a "safe" relationship without the pressure of sex looming overhead at all times. His friend is someone he can safely ask questions of and learn from about how girls feel and think.

 **Alert**

One of the problems with friends who are girls is hooking up. This is an easy way of having a sexual relationship with a girl, supposedly without the strings of a relationship. Talk to your son about his choices and respect for others.

When One Person Wants More

One issue that can arise is that sometimes these opposite-sex friendships wind up with at least one person desiring a physical relationship. This person may or may not be your son.

It is important to talk to your son and teach him about issues like this in friendship and how it can affect the friendship.

If your son is in a relationship like this, talk to him about his options for dealing with the situation. Does he have the crush? If so, he needs to decide if it is best to talk to his friend about his feelings. If he decides it is important to him to let her know, he must have a game plan. What does he want to say? When and how should he say it? Some role-playing with you might be a great way to help him prepare, though he may reject this idea.

You should also explain to him what the benefits and the risks are for this disclosure. He needs to understand that this may ultimately be the end of their friendship. This can happen whether she rejects him outwardly or not. Even if she says "no" to something more than friendship, the friendship may sour from there.

Ⓔ *Question*

Can guys and girls be friends?
Some argue that the laws of physical attraction will always win, and males will want a physical relationship. However, there are plenty of successful male/female relationships that do not get physical.

The same is true if the roles are reversed, and she is the one who has the more intense feelings for your son. She may decide to talk to your son about her feelings and he may or may not accept. But the friendship may ultimately be in danger, even if they agree they can deal with it.

The one big problem is when either party decides to stay friends, but then uses the other's feelings as power. Your son must understand that using these feelings to his advantage is wrong. It is emotional abuse and should not be tolerated. He may be the abuser or abused in this situation. In either situation, counseling is always recommended.

Technical Virginity

Most parents feel pretty clear about the definition of virginity. Teens have a completely different concept of the word.

What Is Virginity?

Many teen boys define virginity purely as vaginal penetration with a penis. All other forms of sexual contact are fair play. This can include oral sex and anal sex.

Oral sex is an easy way to claim to be a technical virgin. In a 2005 study, just over half of the fifteen- to nineteen-year-olds had already experienced oral sex. One in four of the teens who had not had intercourse had oral sex.

 *Essential*

Teaching your son about the joy and love that come along with the responsibility of sex is part of your job. Be sure he knows about the female anatomy and the art of female orgasm.

Some teens describe oral sex as being much less intimate than sexual intercourse. Oral sex was once considered much more intimate than sexual intercourse. Today's teens do not know what to think and therefore they need you to weigh in on the matter to help them make their own decisions.

What Your Son Needs to Know

One of the biggest problems with the whole issue of technical virginity is not who has the correct definition. The biggest concern is really that most teens do not understand the risks involved with sexual contact of any sort. The truth is that anal, oral, and vaginal sex or contact with any sex organs can lead to problems other than pregnancy.

 Alert

Plan B (*www.go2planb.com*). It's more than an alternate plan— it's emergency birth control. Plan B is most effective within three days of unprotected or less-than-ideally protected intercourse.

Many teen boys claim that if you avoid penile/vaginal sex then you can also avoid some of the hazards associated with this form of sexual contact. This is absolutely a false assumption. There are many risks involved with other forms of sexual contact.

It is important that your son know that any form of sexual contact can lead to sexually transmitted infections, also know as sexually transmitted diseases (STDs) or venereal diseases.

Your son should know the common symptoms of sexually transmitted infections:

- Pain during urination or sex
- Discharge from the penis
- Sores in the genital region, anus, or mouth
- Swollen glands
- General fatigue

Teach your son options for sexual outlet. Outercourse is the act of sexual rubbing with clothes, also known as dry humping. This is one way to release sexual tension with none of the physical risks related to sex.

Dating Violence

Dating violence is an issue you need to raise with your son. Dating violence can be the emotional, physical, or sexual abuse of a dating partner.

Dates Gone Wrong

Studies show that one in three women have been victims of violence at the hands of their dates. This is a huge problem for your son, because he needs to be sure that he is not one of the abusers. Such violence is rarely reported because teens have little experience with intimate relationships and don't know how to respond to problems.

It is more likely to happen if your son is showing some of the following signs:

- Jealousy
- A need to control his date
- Keeping her away from friends or peers
- Problems with anger
- Violent behavior at home or school
- Other emotional issues
- Previous threatening or violent behavior

If your son has problems like this, he should seek help before dating. If you learn of such behavior after the fact, then seek help immediately. Your son needs your help to identify this problem if he is experiencing trouble because he may not see it as an issue.

Power, Not Sex

Date rape and other forms of sexual violence are not about sex. They are about power over someone else. In an attempt to control or exert power over someone else, sexual acts are often used.

Ⓔ *Fact*

Talking to your son about dating violence is very important. The Centers for Disease Control and Prevention offer a free brochure to aid you in these discussions at *www.cdc.gov/ncipc/dvp/SVPrevention.htm*.

No Means No

One of the best things that you can teach your son is that "no" means no. This goes for his voice and the voice of those he dates. This is not just about sexual intercourse but anything. He should know that he should never be forced to do something he does not want to do, and that he should never force anyone into doing something he or she doesn't want to do.

Role-playing can be very helpful with this type of lesson. Show him what "no" can look like, because it can take on many different forms. Teach him to look for the "no," even when he wants to see the "yes." Things like flirtatious behavior and scantily clad bodies are not invitations to have sex. While there may be a lot of peer pressure to have sex, it is okay not to "score."

 *Alert*

Rape and sexual assault do not happen only to women. One in ten men is raped. Your son is at risk and needs to know how to protect himself.

It is also important that your son understand that if a girl is drunk or high or otherwise unable to consent to sex, then it is rape. This is true even if your son is also intoxicated. It does not matter if he didn't know she was intoxicated. Rape-proof your son. Teach him that if a girl says "no" or acts like she doesn't want to have sex, he should stop. If she is hesitant, he should stop. If either of them has been drinking, he shouldn't have sex with her. It is not worth the risk to him.

Chapter 14

Coping with
Mental Health Issues
and Problem Behaviors

Try as you might to guarantee that your son grows up safely, adolescents sometimes encounter frightening issues. At these times, they need their parents' love and support more than ever, even when their behavior seems intended to drive you away. You need to use all your resources to identify what is wrong with your son and how to help him.

Identifying Problem Behavior

When faced with raising an adolescent boy, it is likely that you have questioned your sanity as well as your son's normality. Trying to figure out what is normal and what isn't can be a difficult task for any parent. For the parents of teens it is even more difficult.

Normal Behavior of Teens

The teen years are hard on your son. He is experiencing great changes in his body as well as his mind and emotions. This is a time of turmoil for him, and it makes him more volatile in general.

 *Essential*

Sometimes you may find yourself constantly looking out for problems or negative behavior, but your son needs to know when he is doing something right. Find some easy ways to tell him when he's doing a good job, and reward him with something that shows you care.

Your son's job is to assert his independence to define himself. This is usually shown as defiance. He may also show himself to be less capable than he expects, which may lead to some periods of time where he is worried or concerned. He will usually react to these situations with defiance as well.

By being available for your son, you can help him through these rough periods. It also allows you to watch, even from a distance, what he is doing. You can pick up on any clues that he is at risk for greater problems.

Abnormal Behavior of Teens

It can be easy as a parent to bury your head in the sand when your son is behaving unpleasantly. The problem is that when you stop paying attention you can miss some of the signs that your son needs help. These signs might include:

- Defiance to all authority
- Lack of friends
- Withdrawal from all social activity
- Focus on violent books, shows, or characters
- Persistent refusal to do chores and other simple tasks
- Lack of dreams and goals for the future

The difference between normal and not normal can basically be defined as a persistence of the problematic behaviors. You will fight and disagree with your son. This is a given. But if it is a constant battle, there may be some underlying issues going on and you need to seek help. Sometimes it is depression, other times it is a medical condition or even drug abuse. The watchful eye of a parent will pick up these differences and be able to respond and seek care.

Bad Attitude and Negativity

The Parenting Adolescents Web site recently ran a poll where the majority of parents listed attitude as one of the top three concerns for their teens. No matter the reason behind your son's bad attitude, it hurts you as a parent.

Why the Attitude?

Your son may seem to have the attitude that everything you say or do is wrong. He may resist you at every turn. He may just be a naysayer, ignoring everything you propose. This is a common complaint of parents of teen boys. They can't stand the bad attitude and negativity. Many parenting experts say this resistance is all a part of growing up. The attitude represents your son's way of pulling away and resisting your help. He is asserting his independence.

Handling the Attitude

As painful as it is to be on the receiving end, it is important to keep in mind that there really is a purpose. What it boils down to is that parents often feel disrespected when their son is behaving that way.

 Fact

> Keeping your cool while talking to your son is very important. Staying calm while your son is angry sets a good example for him; he will realize you expect the same behavior from him.

You will need to set rules for your son. Explain that testing the boundaries is normal and expected, but that disrespecting you is not acceptable. Point out how he can "rebel" within these guidelines. For example, you want him to do his homework, and he wants to go out with his friends. He can stomp off, call you names and slam the door, asserting that he will not do his homework. This is unacceptable. Explain that a more reasonable alternative would be to tell you his plan to get his homework done while still finding time for his friends. This allows him to be respectful while asserting his right to do his homework on his schedule. Role-play to help you both understand your positions, and when you disagree in real life, you will both know how to act.

ADHD and ADD

Attention-deficit hyperactivity disorder (ADHD) is a much-discussed subject for parents. From discussing the possibilities of your child having it to dealing with other kids with ADHD at school, it's likely that ADHD directly affects your son, if not you. Therefore, it is important to learn what you can do to help your son. The National Institute of Mental Health (NIMH) suggests that between 3 and 5 percent of children have ADHD.

Diagnosing ADHD

Maybe a teacher told you she suspects your son has ADHD, or perhaps another parent looked at you and said, "Oh yes, it's definitely ADHD. I'd know it anywhere." Attention-deficit hyperactivity disorder (ADHD) is defined by the American Psychiatric Association (APA) as having three subtypes:

- Primarily inattentive
- Primarily impulsive
- Combined type (impulsive and inattentive)

However, there is only one way to know for sure if your son has ADHD. He must be evaluated by a qualified specialist with a background in ADHD. Other practitioners may guess and offer a prescription, but it could be a misdiagnosis. Bipolar disorder, substance abuse, and other problems may present as ADHD, which is why you need someone who will do a full inspection of your son and his history, including physical, mental, and emotional outlook, school work, and social life.

Helping the ADHD Adolescent Boy

Once your son has been diagnosed with ADHD, you may feel relieved. You have a diagnosis, and now you can move forward with a specific set of rules that will help. Many parents quickly become disillusioned with the wide variety of help available, from medications to behavior modification. The truth is that finding what works for your son may take time, and trial and error.

 Fact

Oppositional defiance disorder is defined by the American Academy of Child and Adolescent Psychiatry as the exhibiting of an "ongoing pattern of uncooperative, defiant, and hostile behavior toward authority figures that seriously interferes with the youngster's day to day functioning."

You can use your health care provider to assist you, as well as a specialist who focuses on ADHD. You will hopefully be able to successfully involve your child's school to help resolve the issues or symptoms that you son is experiencing. This can be a challenge, but your son is protected under the Americans with Disabilities Act (ADA), and the school is required to help. Be sure you know your rights.

As a teen, your son can be helpful in verbalizing what works and what doesn't. Use this to your advantage; it is something younger children often have a problem doing. Help your son's doctor monitor his medication, which may need adjustments because of his changing physical nature. Your son may weigh more and need more medication or he may have better control over impulses as he ages and need less medications. Stay in close contact with your son and with those you have assisting your family.

Lying

No one likes to be told a lie. That said, your son will probably lie to you at some point in your career as a parent. If it's more or less expected, is it a problem? When does lying become an issue that needs to be addressed?

What Is a Lie?

Most teens believe that there is more to life than the truth—and here's the kicker, they don't really think they are lying either. There is some gray area that includes half-truths, fibs, evasion of the facts, and other not-so-honest answers to even the simplest of questions.

This can make your life as a parent very difficult when it comes to figuring out what the truth is and what isn't.

E *Essential*

Telling the truth can sometimes hurt. This doesn't mean that honesty isn't the best policy—but it does mean that you might have to teach your son that it is acceptable to feel uncomfortable when telling the truth.

Telling the truth and being honest boils down to trust. To break the trust between you and your son is a slap in the face. The real key is to try to figure out the reason behind the lie. Is he lying to try to stay out of trouble? Is he lying to be able to do something he knows you won't give permission for? Is he lying to make himself seem better or more interesting to someone? Each lie may have a different root problem.

How to Confront a Lie

The first and most important step when addressing lying is to do it immediately. Do not wait to confront your son or the power may be lost. Remain calm and firm. You do not need to tell him how you know he is lying, only that you do. He may try to stand his ground and insist that his story is the correct version, even when you know it is not.

 *Essential*

If you are having an ongoing problem with lying, try to consider where the lie starts. Getting to the root of the problem will help solve it more effectively than repeatedly punishing repeated lies.

Before jumping straight to the punishment, you should try to talk to your son. If you can figure out why he is lying then perhaps you can better help address the issues that may be behind the lies. Once you are done talking, remind him of the punishment previously agreed upon. Let him know that he will also have to re-earn your trust. One way for him to do this is to be accountable in everything, volunteering information about where he is going and how his schoolwork is progressing.

Stealing

Stealing is a crime. The person who steals, no matter how small or insignificant the item seems, is still a thief. As a parent, your policy should be that stealing of any sort is not appropriate.

What Is Stealing?

When you talk about stealing, shoplifting is probably your first thought. While this is the most common form of stealing outside the home for teens to participate in, this is not typically where stealing starts. Stealing usually starts at home and when children are much younger.

 Fact

Kleptomania is an uncommon disorder where a person steals repeatedly. The person might not even realize that he or she is stealing; some do it just because they can. If you think your son has kleptomania, seek professional help for him.

Your son may borrow something from your closet or pick up a sibling's toy and use it as his own. These are minor forms of stealing. Your son may try to pass it off as legitimate borrowing, but it is not borrowing unless your son has permission.

You need to explain to your son that any form of stealing will not be tolerated and assign appropriate forms of discipline. Having a strict stance and immediate reaction can hopefully spare your son some pain in the future as the stakes get higher.

Shoplifting

Shoplifting is defined as someone stealing something out of a store. While stores have done their best to deter shoplifting with signs, security cameras, security officers, and security tags, it still happens. Many teenagers are shoplifting for the sheer thrill of it, not because they can't have the product or need the product.

E Alert

Stealing may be a symptom of a larger problem. If your son has other problems, including substance abuse, he may steal to get money, drugs, or alcohol. He may steal money from you at home or from others. He needs professional help.

Many teens think of shoplifting as a game. Some believe that taking a five-dollar item from a huge chain store is not stealing and hurts no one. The truth is that shoplifting is not a victimless crime, and everyone pays the price for shoplifters, no matter how small. Your son may feel pressure to shoplift. His friends may do it and encourage him to do so as well. It can be hard for him to resist this peer pressure, and he certainly doesn't want to be called a chicken in front of his friends, so he may steal to save face.

Make sure that your son understands the consequences of stealing. He may go to jail. He may have a record of his crime for the rest of his life, which may prevent him from getting into the college he wants or from getting a job later down the road.

Violence

No parent wants to think of his or her son as violent, and yet at some point every child and teen will be aggressive or violent.

What Is Violence?

Aggression is at the core of violent behavior. Aggression stems from attempts to control the environment and the people in it. The problems begin when your son is aggressive in a manner that shows disregard for other people, their feelings, and their property.

 Fact

Violence breeds a whole realm of other unsavory behaviors. Teens who take part in acts of violence tend to be involved in other problematic things. Violence is not something that happens alone or in a vacuum.

Violence and aggression might look like a series of nasty behaviors including verbal abuse, physical abuse, destruction of property, and the like. If left uninterrupted, violence will become a predictable coping mechanism. This is when it becomes a problem.

How to Handle Violence

To stem the tide of violence in your son, you need to step in at the early signs and provide your son with a correct and appropriate way to handle pressure and situations where he may typically feel like being violent. One of the best ways to do this is to show your son the difference between aggression and assertiveness.

Being assertive is a positive alternative to being aggressive. It allows your son to stand up for himself and have some control over his environment but without the negative effects on those near him. Role-playing also works well here. Show your son how to respond to normal situations he may face regularly, without violence. He may not even realize the problem he is having.

Depression and Suicide

Depression and suicide are very scary concepts for parents to contemplate, yet many teens live with depression and/or think about suicide. Your support as a parent can make a huge difference in your son's life.

Depression

Depression is more than occasionally feeling sad or blue. It is typically something that lasts more than a week or two. It can start as a normal reaction to a situation or it can simply begin.

Depression in teens may be similar to that in adults. They may stop participating in social activities, even with good friends. A depressed teen may let his appearance and grades slip. However, depressed teens may not always appear sad. Depressed teens may instead be angry and irritable, or have significant anxiety or fears. These are all signs of a problem. Though not every teen shows a set series of signs, be sure you are looking for changes in your son so you can help when needed.

E *Fact*

There are many mental health disorders that look like depression to the untrained eye. It is important for your son to have a correct diagnosis from a qualified mental health practitioner.

Suicide

Suicide among teens is relatively rare, but is an issue all parents must be aware of. Although the numbers are changing somewhat, teen girls more frequently attempt suicide, but teen boys are actually more likely to die from a suicide attempt. This is because teen boys tend to choose more lethal methods of suicide.

Suicide is the third leading cause of death in teens. While it is often associated with other mental health disorders, including depression, bipolar disorder, and other illnesses, it can also be spontaneous. Frequently, suicides occur near specific instances like a romantic breakup, the death of a relative or friend, school problems, copycat suicides, and other problems that may come up quickly.

 *Alert*

There is a National Suicide Hotline available twenty-four hours a day, seven days a week at 1-800-SUICIDE. The hotline was established in 1999 as part of the Kristin Brooks Hope Center. You can also read more about suicide, depression, and helping those who are affected at its Web site: *www .hopeline.com.*

Talk to your son about depression and suicide, even if he shows no signs of either depression or suicidal thoughts. This will show him you care and that he can approach you about these issues. If your son is uncomfortable talking to you, have him talk with another adult, such as a counselor or another family member. You should seek care for your son immediately if you observe any of the following signs:

- Giving away possessions
- Fascination with death in music, drawings, writing, or film
- Sudden loss of relationships (family or friends)
- Stating he wants to die or kill himself
- Plans of suicide
- Symptoms of clinical depression

Many people who are contemplating suicide are not capable of asking for help, so your help as a parent is critical. It is important for your son to get a proper diagnosis so that he can be treated appropriately. Most teens who attempt suicide are also clinically depressed. Many of the causes of disorders that lead to suicidal thoughts and behavior can be treated with therapy and sometimes medications. It is always wise to err on the side of caution.

Living in a Fantasy World

There are days we would all like to escape reality. In a fantasy world, there would be no work, no responsibilities, and lots of things that we consider to be fun. Teens sometimes use their imaginations as a coping mechanism.

 *Essential*

Fantasy novels, mangas, and graphic novels are all a part of the fantasy genre that your son may actively read. Some teachers find this genre is a great way to entice reluctant readers.

What Is a Fantasy?

So your son thinks he's a rock star or a golf pro. Maybe his fantasy revolves around something else, like books or special characters. This is a normal part of being a teen. It's a chance for him to try on different personas and find himself.

Typically you will find an active fantasy life in the younger teen sets, say between age twelve and fourteen. This is not to say that older teens don't have the occasional dream of being somewhere or someone else. The problem is when your teen can't tell real life from his fantasy life. The period of the late teens is a time when schizophrenia may show up. Signs that your son isn't leaving his fantasy world may be early signs of schizophrenia. Be sure to seek professional help to diagnose this disorder.

When the Fantasy Is Harmful

Most of the time trying to be someone else for a few hours at a time is not a bad thing. Everyone has a way of relaxing and getting away from real life. In fact, it is no different from what some adults do with fantasy sports leagues. These are the normal and healthy fantasies.

As your teen gets older, he should be better able to compartmentalize his coping mechanism and separate real life from fantasy. Some boys lose track of this and start to truly believe that their fantasy is reality. This can be a huge issue for parents. If this happens, you need to seek professional help. Your son may have some other issues going on that require assistance.

Chapter 15

Surviving and Thriving During His Adolescence

When all is said and done, your job of raising a young boy through his teen years to be a man is an amazing task. It is not one that is to be taken on lightly. It is truly a gift of love, mixed with some blood, sweat, and tears.

Don't Relive Your Own Adolescence

Many parents inadvertently relive or try to relive their own adolescence through the years their son is living his own adolescence. This is a huge mistake. It will only stand to bring about conflict and feelings of dissatisfaction.

You Had Your Chance

Ah, the joys of being a teen. You probably had some really good times when you were a teen. You may have also had at least a few really bad times—or at least things you wish you could change. This is not your chance.

There are, no doubt, lingering issues that we all have to deal with from our own adolescence. If you have these feelings, you may not know or recognize them until you are in the throes of your son's adolescence. If you find you are experiencing issues of unresolved feelings, guilt, longing, or other odd emotions, you may consider seeking mental health support.

 Fact

> If you had a hard time growing up because of a negative experience or if something feels unresolved, it is absolutely normal to want to spare your son these feelings. The problem is that it doesn't work this way. Your son must live his own life, and you must let him.

Your Son Needs His Turn

You often hear people telling teens to enjoy these years because they are the best of their lives. Teens often think the adults who say this are lying, crazy, or both. But the truth is that there is something unique about being a teen. There is a sense of freedom and safety that you can never quite recapture once you move on.

During these years, your son will take important steps toward being an adult. To skip a step or to be robbed of the experience is a dent in his ability to move forward. Be cognizant of the fact that your son needs to do many things during these years and that you need to let him actually do them; you cannot grow for him.

Letting Go

The truth is that adolescence is just one long goodbye. You will slowly learn to give your son responsibility, and he will learn to take it.

Start the Process Early

There isn't a light switch that goes off at the age of eighteen or when your son graduates from college that pronounces him ready to be an adult. Teens need to be groomed for the real world from an early age. They need to be given small doses of responsibility. Think of these as test doses.

 Alert

You may find you have a few more fights with your son in the months between high school graduation and the start of college, particularly over issues like curfew. Try to deal with this argument before it becomes an issue.

Since the process will take years to master, you have lots of time to teach your son, though toward the end you may feel a sense of panic that your son isn't quite ready.

Try to remember that the time you have left is precious but limited. Consider writing out a list of the things you have left to teach him. Share that list with your son. Let him have a go at making suggestions about what he wants to learn, either on his list or on yours. Remember, just because he goes off to college doesn't mean he can't ever come back.

Let Your Work Speak for Itself

As you let go, you may feel like you're leaving your baby to be devoured by wolves. That is not the case. You have spent the last thirteen-plus years working hard to teach your son things that will help him be a self-reliant and good person.

 Fact

A study by the National Center on Addiction and Substance Abuse shows that in a house that has established rules, teens were less likely to drink or do drugs. Teens also reported better relationships with their parents.

You have built your son's character and taught him the skills he needs to think and live. Now it's time to take a step back and let him go. This means having confidence in yourself as a parent and trusting the work you've been doing for all those years. If you let him go, he will fly as you taught him to do.

Accommodating Changing Interests

Remember when your son was small and you mapped out everything he did? Twenty-four hours a day, seven days a week, you were his tour guide. The best part was that not only did he not complain, he loved it. Simply being with you was a treat, no matter what you did. Now that your son is a teen, chances are you couldn't find something cool to do if your life depended on it—at least in his eyes.

The Key Is Flexibility

You once dictated your son's interests. If you signed him up for soccer or football, he went. As your son started to get older, he probably expressed a preference—not football, just soccer, or soccer here and not there, please. He began to take control of his desires.

Now that your son is a teen, he may have even more to say about what he does. Talk to your son about the activities he wants to do and those he doesn't want to do. Then come up with an acceptable list of rules for choosing activities. Keep the following in mind when choosing:

- Distance from home
- Cost involved
- Skills required
- Time commitment
- Interference with schoolwork

Once you have mapped out the pros and cons of each activity, evaluate which activities are most likely to fit into his schedule. Both of you should be prepared to compromise.

Trying to Find Common Ground

Doing something you and your son both love is probably one of the easiest ways to spend time together. It also can help you when other forms of communication break down; at least you have your weekly golf game or trip to the movies. This can be a bit more difficult as your son grows up.

Since the goal is to find something to do together, you both need to be flexible. As the parent, you may be a bit more open to being flexible, and this can provide a great lesson for your son. One way to show this flexibility and a sense of adventure is to take turns planning things to do together. Before you get started, you may want to set up some ground rules together on these excursions. These rules might be that:

- The cost is under X amount of dollars.
- The excursion cannot involve _____ (list restriction, might be physical limitations).
- There are geographical limitations.

You might try switching off every other month or every few weeks. This is an opportunity for you to try new things and spend time together.

E Fact

Stay involved in your son's life outside of the house. This might mean joining the Parents' Orchestra Association just to be near your son. This lets you see what's going on in his life and allows you to show him you are taking an interest in helping him, even if you don't do it side by side.

When choosing activities, consider where you will be and what you will be doing. Will there be time to talk if desired? Will you be sitting and not interacting (movies) or moving around and chatting (hiking)? These are things to keep in mind when scheduling your weeks.

Avoiding Conflict

Conflict may seem to increase as your son gets older. This is his attempt to pull away and be on his own. The conflict and situations that arise from it are not pleasant for anyone.

The Ground Rules

While you may understand his need for independence, you probably don't enjoy fighting about it. Remind him that you aren't the enemy and that he doesn't need to fight you for the right to breathe.

Ⓔ *Essential*

If you are looking for practical advice and a friendly group of parents to talk to or meet with, check out the Parenting of Adolescents Web site (*www.parentingteens.about.com*).

As tensions rise, communications break down and emotions come into play. This is where it can get really nasty and ugly. The problem is that the love between you and your son makes everything seem worse.

Fighting fairly is important, but so is understanding. While using active listening skills, be sure you try to understand the situation from your son's perspective. This means you also get a chance to help him see your point of view as well.

Privileges Versus Rights

One of the biggest sources of conflict is something your son believes he deserves and sees as a right. The problem? You see it as a privilege that he hasn't yet earned.

A right is something that no bad behavior can take away. Rights include food, shelter, clothing, and other necessities. The ability to drive the family car is not a right, nor is money to go out with his friends. This is often a difficult lesson.

This is a discussion to have early and often so that your son understands the concept, though sometimes his emotions will take over and he will feel more inclined to actually ignore what his brain is saying. This is normal and to be expected.

The understanding of rights versus privileges will also help to resolve conflicts. This distinction makes it easier to explain your point of view, and it removes the emotion from the conflict when you boil it down to this simple issue. Your son will eventually learn to remove his emotions from the conflict.

Rescuing Your Son

Watching failure is painful. This is not what you thought you signed up for, and yet you know how important it is for your son to fail in order to grow.

Lifeguard Duty

When your son was little, your job was to keep him safe. You installed safety gates to keep him from falling down the stairs. You took him to have his immunizations to prevent nasty diseases. You fed him, loved him, and kept him safe and healthy. The good news is that your job description has not changed a bit—what has changed is how you do your job.

Ⓔ *Essential*

Your son has a huge fear that you will not love him. Of all the lifeguard duties you have, be sure he always knows you love him. Your actions speak louder than words. A quick hug on a daily basis, even if he pretends to pull away, should help.

Now that your son is an adolescent, you probably aren't worried about him falling down the stairs as much as you worry about him trying drugs. You want him to get good grades to help him in the future, but you can't make him do it. This is where you need to learn to practice selective rescuing.

What this means is that your son will be in charge of many of his decisions. Your job is still to keep him healthy, love him, feed him, and keep him safe. Now you need to really think about safety. Step in when certain criteria are involved, such as the following:

- His life is in danger
- He will cause irreparable harm to himself or others
- He will damage something that belongs to someone else

You may be a guiding force, but you must let your son have the final say in more of the decisions in his life.

Not Quite Ready to Leave Home

Eighteen or high school graduation. They are not the magical times for all boys. Some teen boys are simply not yet ready for the real world at these milestones. This doesn't make them bad kids, or you a bad parent. It makes you a realist. This is a decision that you and your son need to make together.

E *Fact*

You can't really stop your son from leaving home at eighteen, short of a court order for a really intense issue like mental illness. This is why you need to have your son's buy-in on the extended length of stay at home. A contract works well.

If you find yourself in this situation, counseling can be healthy for everyone involved. It may also help you find a path to help your son get the extra skills that he needs to move on.

This may be an issue of academics. Preparing for college by attending junior or community college can be a big help. Your son may also simply need to learn some responsibility, and a job might be helpful. This is not a permanent situation but rather an extra opportunity. Simply leaving home because he can may not be the best choice.

Refocusing Your Energies

Now that your son is preparing to leave the house, you have a lot more time on your hands. What will you do with it?

Surviving the Nest

Even if you don't have a completely empty nest, having a child grow up and leave home will make a dent in your life. You know it's a good thing for your son to get out and find his own way in the world, but it doesn't make his absence from your daily life any less jarring. Acknowledge your own emotional state. You may also feel many different emotions on the same day. It is all a part of the growth process.

Ⓔ *Essential*

> Now that you and your spouse have less to focus on, you may realize you have both changed since you met, married, and had children. Use this time to strengthen your relationship and discover one another anew.

The key to surviving a changing nest is to be honest with yourself. By knowing you may have a variety of feelings and giving yourself permission to have them, you will move more quickly into a new normal for your life. If you find you are experiencing more sadness or having trouble thinking of anything else, it may be time to seek some counseling. Sometimes just having a place to talk will help you sort through your feelings.

Focus on Other Relationships

When your son leaves home, you now have more time to focus on other relationships in your life. You may be able to nurture old relationships that may have been neglected as you focused on parenting. You can cultivate new relationships with others as you move forward into a new part of your life.

Essential

> One way to nurture your body and soul is to use your extra time to focus on yourself. You can take classes, either for fun or for a degree. You will find ways to enjoy yourself, even while your son is on your mind.

You will fill your time with new or renewed relationships once your son needs less attention. This can be an exciting time for you. You may find that you crave the ability to meet new people. You and your spouse may decide to do something fun like take a class together or start a garden. Perhaps you have a list of projects or places to travel that you've been saving in a file for when your son was moving away. Now is your chance.

Relationships are important in your life. Your son is not being pushed aside. You are taking care of yourself as your son would want you to do, and just as you would tell your son to do in a similar situation.

Seeing Your Son as a Man

It doesn't seem like so long ago that your newborn baby was placed in your arms. Before you knew it, there was a toddler running around, and then suddenly your son was standing on a school bus waving goodbye. Now he's wearing a cap and gown and shaving—and preparing to go off and leave home.

How Did That Happen?

You've spent approximately the last eighteen years nurturing your son. You've shown him what it means to be a man and a good person. You've argued about music, friends, schoolwork, and lots of other issues. Now he's ready to step out on his own.

 Fact

Chronological age doesn't equal maturity. Some studies show that teen boys may mature a bit more slowly than their female counterparts, but in the end, remember that most teens who leave home do wind up doing all right despite the rough start.

You've given it your best shot. Don't look backward and think of things you could have done; focus on your great accomplishment—your son. As his parent, you get to watch him continue to grow and do great things.

A New Relationship

Focus on the great job you've done, not the scary things that are potentially still out there. Know that you are always there for your son; more importantly, be sure that your son also knows that. Have a plan for what to do if he wants or needs help.

You and your son will learn to adjust to the new relationship, even if you see each other less frequently. This is not the end of the road for you and your son. It is merely a change in the relationship. If your son is going away to school or moving for a job, you will have to learn to stay in touch with each other. Thankfully, there are many really neat ways to do this, including:

- E-mail
- Blogging
- Cell phones (with lots of free minutes)
- Snail mail (but don't hold your breath!)

 Alert

Don't let your son leave before discussing practicalities with him. Discuss where he will live and how he will pay rent. Since your son has never had to pay bills and utilities on his own, he may not realize everything he needs to do.

When the day comes for your son to leave, remember to focus on what's going on and not the emotions of it all. While you both feel the emotions, it is important to minimize them, because you are probably feeling a confusing mix of emotions. Help him move into the dorm or apartment, give him a big hug, and remind him that you are always there for him, no matter what. Then shut the door and go home, leaving your son to his bright future, where you will play a smaller but still vital part in his life.

Appendix A

Resources

These resources are designed to help you on your journey as you parent your adolescent son. Some of these books are meant to be shared with your son, while others are meant for your reading or his reading alone. The same holds true for the Web sites and other resources. It's a handy list to have around, particularly the crisis hotlines. So many things about being a teen feel like a crisis, even to an even-tempered teen.

Be sure you read the information in books or Web sites before recommending them to your son. You know your son well and will be able to have a good sense of which resources are best for him. You might also be surprised to find your son has a list of places for you to check out as well.

Books

American Heart Association. *Fitting in Fitness: Hundreds of Simple Ways to Put More Physical Activity into Your Life.* (Clarkson Potter; reissue edition, 1997)

Bodenhamer, Gregory. *Parent in Control: Restore Order in Your Home and Create a Loving Relationship with Your Adolescent.* (Fireside, 1995)

Carlson, Richard. *Don't Sweat the Small Stuff for Teens.* (Hyperion, 2000)

Chapman, Gary. *The Five Love Languages of Teenagers.* (Northfield Publishing, 2000)

Covey, Sean. *The 6 Most Important Decisions You'll Ever Make: A Guide for Teens.* (Fireside, 2006)

————. *The 7 Habits of Highly Effective Teens.* (Fireside, 1998)

Faber, Adele, and Elaine Mazlish. *How to Talk So Kids Will Listen and Listen So Kids Will Talk (How to Help Your Child).* (Piccadilly Press Ltd.; new edition, 2001)

Frankel, Viktor. *Man's Search for Meaning.* (Beacon Press; 1st edition, 2006)

Graham, Stedman. *Teens Can Make It Happen: Nine Steps to Success.* (Fireside, 2000)

Gurian, Michael. *The Wonder of Boys.* (Tarcher, 2006)

Hallowell, Edward, and John Ratey. *Driven to Distraction: Recognizing and Coping with Attention Deficit Disorder from Childhood Through Adulthood.* (Touchstone; reprint edition, 1995)

Haskins, Diana. *Parent as Coach: Helping Your Teen Build a Life of Confidence, Courage and Compassion.* (White Oak Publishing, 2002)

Hawkins, Frank C., and Greta L. B. Laube, *The Boy's Body Guide: A Health and Hygiene Book for Boys 8 and Older* (Perfect Paperback). (Boys Guide Books; 1st edition, 2007)

Isaacson, Clifford E., and Kris Radish. *The Birth Order Effect: How to Better Understand Yourself and Others.* (Adams Media Corporation, 2002)

Kidd, Kenneth. *Making American Boys: Boyology and the Feral Tale.* (University Of Minnesota Press; Reprint edition, 2005)

Kindlon, Dan, and Michael Thompson. *Raising Cain: Protecting the Emotional Life of Boys.* (Ballantine Books; 1st edition, 2000)

Leman, Kevin. *Bringing Up Kids Without Tearing Them Down: How to Raise Confident, Successful Children.* (Thomas Nelson, 2001)

Levine, Madeline. *The Price of Privilege: How Parental Pressure and Material Advantage Are Creating a Generation of Disconnected and Unhappy Kids.* (HarperCollins, 2006)

Lewis, Barbara, and Pamela Espeland. *What Do You Stand For? For Teens: A Guide to Building Character.* (Fireside, 2000)

Madaras, Lynda, and Area Madaras. *What's Happening to My Body? Book for Boys: A Growing Up Guide for Parents and Sons.* (Newmarket Press, 2000)

Mogel, Wendy. *The Blessing of a Skinned Knee: Using Jewish Teachings to Raise Self-Reliant Children.* (Penguin; reprint edition, 2001).

Muscari, Mary. *Not My Kid: 21 Steps to Raising a Nonviolent Child.* (University of Scranton Press, 2002)

Packer, Alex. *The How Rude! Handbook of Family Manners for Teens: Avoiding Strife in Family Life* (The How Rude! Handbooks for Teens). (Free Spirit Publishing, 2004)

———. *The How Rude! Handbook of Friendship & Dating Manners for Teens: Surviving the Social Scene* (The How Rude! Handbooks for Teens). (Free Spirit Publishing, 2004)

———. *The How Rude! Handbook of School Manners for Teens: Civility in The Hallowed Halls* (The How Rude! Handbooks for Teens). (Free Spirit Publishing, 2004)

———. *How Rude! The Teenagers' Guide to Good Manners, Proper Behavior, and Not Grossing People Out* (The How Rude! Handbooks for Teens). (Free Spirit Publishing, 1997)

Pollack, William, and Mary Pipher. *Real Boys: Rescuing Our Sons from the Myths of Boyhood.* (Owl Books; new foreword edition, 1999)

Seward, Brian, and Linda Bartlett. *Hot Stones and Funny Bones: Teens Helping Teens Cope with Stress and Anger.* (HCI Teens, 2001)

Vogt, Susan. *Raising Kids Who Will Make a Difference: Helping Your Family Live with Integrity, Value Simplicity, and Care for Others.* (Loyola Press, 2002)

Web Sites

Teen Growth
✍ *www.teengrowth.com*
Information all about teen health for teens. From nutrition to teen pregnancy, this site has you covered.

National Center for Learning Disabilities
✍ *www.ncld.org*
Information on getting help for your son's learning disabilities; information on finding local resources and helping your son and his teachers.

Smoking Cessation at About.com
✍ *http://quitsmoking.about.com*
Information on how to quit smoking, including statistics on prevention and cessation.

About Alcoholism & Drug Abuse
✍ *http://alcoholism.about.com*
This site has been around for a very long time, and the breadth of the information covered is amazing. While the topic is not

geared specifically for teens it does include valuable information as well as some teen-specific information.

The Cool Spot
✍ *www.thecoolspot.gov*
Information for teens in a clever style, with anime-type characters and great information on bullying, peer pressure, and more.

Steroid Abuse
✍ *www.steroidabuse.org*
Information about steroid abuse for parents and teens.

Tax Tips for Kids Working
✍ *www.hrblock.com/taxes/tax_tips/tax_planning/kids_firstjob.html*
Tax preparation company H&R Block helps you and your son plan ahead for taxes once he starts working.

Youth Rules! Employment Standards
✍ *www.youthrules.dol.gov/states.htm*
A listing of youth employment rules for the United States.

Fight Hate, Promote Tolerance
✍ *www.tolerance.org*
A great way to find what you need to help your child accept himself and others.

10 Ways to Nurture Tolerance

✑ *www.tolerance.org/parents/tenways.jsp*

Ten quick and easy ways to teach your children about tolerance, for every parent.

The American Academy of Pediatrics Talks Puberty

✑ *www.aap.org/family/puberty.htm*

Puberty broken down by male and female and discussed in a rational and mature way from both a physical and mental perspective.

Parenting Adolescents at About.com

✑ *http://parentingteens.about.com*

This site is aimed at the parents of teens, though it does have some appropriate content for teens. It brings a host of information to nearly every imaginable issue.

Teen Advice at About.com

✑ *http://teenadvice.about.com*

This site is designed with teens in mind. There are message boards, articles, and free newsletters from your guide.

Parents. The Anti-Drug: E-monitoring

✑ *www.theantidrug.com/E-Monitoring/internet-lingo.asp*

A great list of Internet and instant messaging lingo to help you interpret what your child is writing.

Practical Money Skills for Life

✍ http://practicalmoneyskills.com/english/at_home/parents/teens.php

These five easy lessons will help any parent teach their son how to handle money.

Occupational Outlook Handbook

✍ www.bls.gov/oco/

This is an amazing resource for helping your son with his career guidance. Not only does it talk about specific jobs but salaries and how likely that job is to still be around.

The National Youth Violence Prevention Resource Center

✍ http://safeyouth.org

This site is designed with something for everyone. The sections are broken down by parent, teen, provider, and so forth. It covers, bullying, depression, violence, and many other topics.

Safe Teens

✍ http://safeteens.org

This site has a bit of everything on it, but it's teen friendly and well organized. It is also available in Spanish.

Ratings for Parents

✍ www.aap.org/family/ratingsgame.htm

Information on video game, movie, television, and computer game ratings for parents by the American Academy of Pediatrics.

Planned Parenthood

✑ *http://plannedparenthood.org*

This organization provides information on teen pregnancy, birth control, and other matters of sexual health for everyone, including teens.

Testicular Self-Exam (TSE)

✑ *http://adam.about.com/encyclopedia/Testicular-self-examination.htm*

A guide to the self-examination of testicles to help early detection of testicular cancer.

Plan B

✑ *www.go2planb.com*

This site is about emergency birth control, what it is, and how to get it.

Sexual Violence Prevention

✑ *www.cdc.gov/ncipc/dvp/SVPrevention.htm*

Information on prevention of sexual violence for everyone.

Organizations

American Academy of Pediatrics (AAP)

✑ *www.aap.org*

The academic and public face of today's pediatricians. Check references as well as learn about current policy.

Kristin Brooks Hope Center

✎ *www.hopeline.com*

✆ 800-SUICIDE

Toll-free suicide hotlines, complete with information on suicide for families as well as those contemplating suicide.

American Academy of Child and Adolescent Psychiatry

✎ *www.aacap.org*

✆ 202-966-7300

Help for understanding childhood mental illness, including facts for families and finding help in your area.

American Psychological Association

✎ *www.helping.apa.org*

✆ 800-964-2000

Find a psychologist and learn more about how they can help you and your family.

American Psychiatric Nurses Association

✎ *www.apna.org*

✆ 202-367-1133

This site is geared toward professionals, but it does offer an interesting legislative outlook.

Parents, Family and Friends of Lesbians and Gays (PFLAG)

✎ *www.pflag.org*

PFLAG is an organization that helps family and friends of lesbians and gays understand and cope with the changes in their family.

Tough Love

✆ 800-333-1069

A series of books and seminars to help the most troubled teens in your life.

Hotlines

National Center for Missing and Exploited Children

🖑 *www.missingkids.com*

Great information for parents to talk to their kids about, regarding how to stay safe.

National Council on Alcoholism Information

✆ 800-NAC-CALL

Referral service for individuals and families seeking help for drug and alcohol abuse issues.

National Suicide Hotline

🖑 *www.hopeline.com*

✆ 800-SUICIDE

A number to call if you are thinking about suicide or if someone you love is thinking about suicide.

Cocaine Hotline

✆ 800-COCAINE

Information on cocaine abuse and helpful resources.

Overeaters Anonymous
✍ *www.oa.org*

Information on overeating support groups and basic information on finding the support you need.

National Association of Anorexia Nervosa and Associated Disorders
✍ *www.altrue.net/site/anadweb/*

Information on eating disorders and finding help.

National Domestic Violence Hotline
✍ *www.ndvh.org*

Information on the prevention of domestic violence and help for those suffering from it.

National Clearing House for Alcohol and Drug Information
✍ *http://ncadi.samhsa.gov*

📞 800-SAY-NOTO

An up-to-date resource for drug information to keep your teen knowledgeable.

Narcotics Anonymous
✍ *http://na.org*

Information for people who are or who know someone addicted to narcotics.

American Council for Drug Education
✍ *www.acde.org*

Educational information for families and teachers.

Al-Anon and Alateen

✐ *www.al-anon.org*

Information to help support teens and families affected by alcohol abuse.

Alcoholics Anonymous

✐ *www.aa.org*

Information on the twelve-step program for helping people kick the alcohol habit.

NIDA Hotline

✆ 800-622-HELP

Referral service for cocaine users.

National HIV Testing Resources

✐ *www.hivtest.org*

A national resource to help you find a testing source near you as well as promote AIDS/HIV education.

Sites You Should Check Out Before Your Son Does

Not every Web site on the Internet is meant for kids. These sites usually act as gateways for meeting others online or revealing private information. Remember to stress the online safety rules to your son, but in the meantime set up an account for yourself on these sites to look for your son and your son's friends to prevent danger.

MySpace

✑ *www.myspace.com*

MySpace is the ideal spot as far as your teen son is concerned. It is free and easy to use. He doesn't need to know any HTML or other programming languages, and he can easily find his friends online. Problems arise when your son posts inappropriate material, knowingly, or unknowingly.

Facebook

✑ *www.facebook.com*

While Facebook is the same kind of site as MySpace in that it is a social networking site, Facebook tends to be a bit cleaner and more academic-minded. Your son still has the ability to add friends, post information, and hook up with others through an online network, but this site doesn't have the same crowd as MySpace.

Social Networking Sites

✑ *http://en.wikipedia.org/wiki/List_of_social_networking_websites*

Social networking is very popular, and there are many subspecialties involved. While MySpace and Facebook are by far the most popular, they are not the only place you will find teens today. The Wikipedia Web site will give you the most up-to-date list of sites, broken down by users as well as the topics they specialize in.

Appendix B

Ten Conversations to Have with Your Son

There are numerous things you likely want to tell your son. Many of them have already been covered in the book. However, it is imperative that the following ten conversations to take place. Remember that how and when you talk is just as important as what you say.

1. Picking a Career Versus a Job

Almost anyone can get a job, and a job can be a very wonderful thing. It can provide you with money to spend on important things like rent, heat, electricity, and food. It can help teenagers pay for car insurance or movies.

The problem is that a job isn't all it's cracked up to be for the long haul, other than paying for necessities. Most people are much happier in a career or following a passion. Teach your son the difference between a career and a job.

Your son needs to know that sometimes on his way to a career, a job is a necessity. He needs to know how to decide what his passion is and how to turn it into a career. This includes what subjects to take in high school, picking a major in college, and how to spend his free time in order to make his dreams come true.

A true passion often leads to a rewarding career. Your son should try to do different things to see what he likes. There are also great programs, tests, and books to help him along the way. Many high schools and some colleges offer programs to help students explore options.

2. Unconditional Love

Your son wants your love. He's always wanted it; from the time he was a small boy, you have been the person he's looked up to and wanted attention and love from. This isn't going to change as he grows up. What does change is that you aren't always around to give him the attention and love he needs because he's not always home or he makes choices that are not great. This all leaves him feeling left in parent-love limbo.

Even when your son has left home, remind him of that you love him. Send him a random card or note that simply says you're thinking of him and love him. This kind of love is difficult to come by and yet so important.

3. Living with Purpose

Purpose is what should drive your life. It helps motivate you and helps make life worth living. Letting external factors dictate your purpose doesn't work because purpose has to come from within. This can be very difficult for parents and teens to understand. Part of it, for parents, is letting go and letting your child explore his own dreams and desires. Let your son know he has a purpose. He is the only one who can determine his purpose and use it to fulfill his life.

4. Your Experience with Drugs and Alcohol

You may think you need to come clean about your personal use of drugs and alcohol or talk about your teen exploits. This really depends on you and your son. Sometimes confession may feel good for the soul, but your son may not be able to handle it. Part of this also depends on your personal story.

You don't necessarily need to go into deep detail, but the general gist of it might be best. It may be difficult to admit to your son that you did some things in your life that weren't the brightest or that you made decisions you now wish you could change. But it also shows your son that you are a human being and don't do everything right all the time either. This is painful for many parents to admit, but it is important for your son to hear. Believe it or not, he probably idolizes you.

Remember that the discussion of drugs and alcohol is not a one-time talk. Such discussions should start early and happen often. It's often something said at just the right time that clicks, even if it wasn't a time you were intentionally trying to make a point.

When you're having these conversations with your son, remember that he thinks differently than you do. First of all, he feels indestructible. Secondly, he can't really think too far into the future. In his mind he will always be young and healthy. Bad things don't happen to him or to people he knows. This is why arguments about drugs often fall flat on teen ears.

Remind your son of your stance and no-tolerance policy. Also remind him that you will do whatever you can to keep him safe and that you are only a phone call away. This means no matter what time or where you are, you are a safe ride.

5. How to Drive a Stick Shift

Before he leaves home, your son needs to know about cars—and not just how to identify one or talk about the hottest model. He needs to know how to drive and how to handle basic car repairs, and to understand basic insurance pointers.

Your son should learn these things even if he doesn't have a driver's license. He needs to know at least the following:

- How to drive both a manual and an automatic
- Car-insurance basics, including the difference between comprehensive and liability insurance
- The importance of manufacturer-recommended maintenance
- How to check the oil, and when and where to get it changed, if he can't do it himself
- How to put windshield-wiper fluid in the car
- How to find and change a spare tire
- How to fill the gas tank
- Where to find his insurance information in the vehicle
- What to do if there is an accident, including whom to call

Hopefully the car won't be a big source of problems between your son and your family. He may love to drive or he may hate it, but he needs to have a basic understanding of what's going on.

6. The Facts of Life: Money

Money is a currency that your son needs to speak fluently to do well in today's world. He needs to know not only how to make money but how to spend it wisely. This means having discussions about budgeting, credit, and saving.

Budget is not a four-letter word. A budget is something to help your son keep track of his money, and sticking to one is every bit as important as balancing a checkbook register. This can prevent frantic calls from your son trying to explain negative bank balances and bouncing checks.

Credit card companies are likely to approach your son as soon as he turns eighteen—and sometimes even earlier. The key is going to be what you've taught him about credit.

Most financial experts agree that Americans in general don't save enough. It is your job to impress upon your son the benefits of savings. Sit down with him and draw it out. How much money he can save may vary, but even when he isn't making a lot of money, $25 saved per paycheck can add up.

7. Showing Emotion

Real men do cry. It's important that you explain this to your son. Growing up without the benefit of being around men who are open about their emotions can lead to many issues for your son. It can also hinder many of his relationships in the future because of his inability to share his emotions with others. Repressing emotions can also be physically and emotionally harmful. Emotionally, you can suffer from stress, which might lead to actual physical illnesses like ulcers and other stress-related illnesses. It can also lead to inappropriate behaviors, like problems with anger.

8. People Versus Stuff

In this day and age, there is stuff everywhere. The accumulation of things is seen as tantamount to almost anything else in life. It is very easy to get carried away with the gathering up of stuff.

Your son needs stuff (cell phone, computer, the right clothes) to be popular with his friends. It is important to make sure he understands that stuff won't make him happy or popular or content; these feelings do not derive from materials goods but from being a good person and helping others.

It isn't wrong to want material objects. The key is to not be focused on them. When your son wants a special object, make him earn it. That will likely attach some physical and mental value to the object. Your son may think, "I really love my new iPod because I worked all summer mowing lawns to earn it."

It is also wise to teach your son that people are not objects. He can't trade people for things and vice versa. He should treat people with respect in every interaction. Remind him to ask how he would want to be treated when the right answer doesn't come automatically.

This can also lead to a discussion about using people. It's wrong to be a friend to someone only to get concert tickets or to be near someone else. This constitutes using the person and abusing their friendship. The same goes with physical benefits. Dating someone for a physical or sexual relationship doesn't make for a great relationship. It robs both people of something important.

9. You!

The past is fascinating. Your son will be naturally curious about what your life was like when you were growing up. While he doesn't want to hear the typical "When I was your age . . . " lectures or how you walked to school uphill both ways in the snow with no shoes, he probably does want to hear what you did for fun, what you thought about friends, life, and growing up.

He may ask you what you thought your life would be like. Be honest with him, even if you aren't doing what you expected to be doing at this point in your life. This is the kind of honesty he looks for in his parents.

Talking to your son about your past is the perfect opportunity to pass on traditions. These small things that mean so much are easily lost. Some of these traditions will surround your family holidays or religious holidays. Birthdays are also times when many traditions occur. Try to live them with your child. Sit down and write them all out; this can actually make a very nice gift for a graduation or a wedding.

Your son many want to know all about your relationship as his parents. He may have questions that you may or may not want to answer. The benefit of sharing your personal story with him is more than mere personal history for him; it provides him with the details of love in a personal context. Your story is more important for him to hear than the stories of love and sex portrayed on television and in music and movies.

Share with your son how you met. What did you feel for each other? Was it love at first sight or did love grow slowly? Talk about the romance. When did you realize you were in love? How did you share this realization with each other? Were the feelings reciprocated? Physically what happened? This might get a bit uncomfortable, so go slowly and share only what feels appropriate.

Talk to your son about how your experiences have shaped what you say to him about love and life. It might really surprise your son to hear such an honest opinion of love in someone he knows. It is also okay to talk to him about the reality of a failed relationship, as long as you are honest with him. This isn't the time or place to bash his other parent; it is simply a statement of the truth. If this is done in a kind and loving way, he can grow and learn from this relationship.

Love can be one of the toughest things to learn about without experiencing it yourself. It is also good to hear a factual account of real-life love. Kids are often overwhelmed when the reality of romance doesn't match the movies. Be sure to talk to them about the morning after the wedding, not just the wedding itself.

10. Having Kids

Your son might think you expect him to grow up and be a parent just like you are. First of all, tell him it is completely his decision. Not everyone has children; some people remain childless, either by choice or because of life circumstances. Talk about how he feels toward parenting in general. Is it something he plans on?

If he plans on being a parent, talk to him about his ideal parent. Let him know that you are aware of the fact that you made mistakes. Let him know that you recognize he will have his own parenting style and make decisions that will be different from those you made.

Tell him about pregnancy—the decision to become pregnant or the shock and surprise you felt when you learned you were going to be a parent. Talk to him about making the decision and enjoying those moments. Talk to him about how important parenting is and how it starts before birth.

Talk to him about how you feel about grandparenting. Tell him what you hope to share with him and his potential children. Let him know that you will love him no matter what he decides to do.

Index